Tales of the Taoist Immortals

Books by Eva Wong

Cultivating Stillness
Cultivating the Energy of Life
Feng-shui
Harmonizing Yin and Yang
Holding Yin, Embracing Yang
Lieh-tzu
A Master Course in Feng-shui
Nourishing the Essence of Life
The Pocket Tao Reader
Seven Taoist Masters
The Shambhala Guide to Taoism
Tales of the Dancing Dragon: Stories of the Tao
Tales of the Taoist Immortals
Teachings of the Tao

Tales of the
Taoist Immortals

Told by
Eva Wong

SHAMBHALA
Boston & London
2001

SHAMBHALA PUBLICATIONS, INC.
Horticultural Hall
300 Massachusetts Avenue
Boston, Massachusetts 02115
www.shambhala.com

9   8   7   6   5   4   3

Printed in the United States of America

♾ This edition is printed on acid-free paper that meets the
American National Standards Institute z39.48 Standard.
Distributed in the United States by Random House, Inc.,
and in Canada by Random House of Canada Ltd

Library of Congress Cataloging-in-Publication Data

Wong, Eva, 1951–
      Tales of the Taoist immortals / Eva Wong.
         p.   cm.
      Includes index.
      ISBN 978-1-57062-809-2 (pbk.)
      1. Gods, Taoist.   2. Mythology, Chinese.   I. Title.
   BL1923.W66   2001
   299′.514213—dc21   00-067964

Contents

Introduction   I

I. THE EIGHT IMMORTALS

   1. The Guest of the Cavern: Lü Tung-pin   II

   2. Hermit of the Cloud Chamber:
      Chungli Ch'uan   16

   3. The Patron of Female Taoists: Ho Hsien-ku   19

   4. The Bat Spirit: Chang Kuo Lao   22

   5. The Immortal with the Iron Crutch:
      T'ieh-kuai Li   26

   6. A Faithful Nephew: Han Hsiang   28

   7. The Wandering Minstrel: Lan Ts'ai-ho   31

   8. The Hermit Aristocrat: Ts'ao Kuo-chiu   33

II. SAGES

   9. The Father of Ch'i-Kung: Chen Hsi-yi   37

  10. Satirist of the High and Mighty:
      Chuang Tzu   42

  11. The Minister and the Courtesan: Fan Li and
      Hsi Shih   45

  12. The Yellow Emperor: Huang Ti   50

  13. The Old One: Lao Tzu   55

  14. A Prince among Taoists: Liu An   57

  15. The Hermit of Mount T'ien-tai:
      Ssu-ma Ch'eng-chen   61

  16. Minister from the Mountains:
      T'ao Hung-ching   65

  17. The First Disciple of Taoism: Wen Shih   70

III. MAGICIANS

18. The Celestial Teacher: Chang Tao-ling   77

19. The Wandering Healer: Fei Chang-fang   82

20. The Sorcerer Strategist: Kiang Tzu-ya   89

21. The Immortal in Sheep's Clothing: Tso Chi   95

22. The Spirit Catcher: Ko Hsüan   98

23. The People's Protector:
    Mah Ku   102

24. Lady of the Great Mysteries: T'ai-hsüan Nü   105

25. The Woman Who Flew on a Toad:
    T'ang Kuang-chen   108

26. Immortal from the Sky: Tung-fang Shuo   111

IV. DIVINERS

27. The Reader of Human Destiny:
    Chang Chung   117

28. The Crane Immortal: Ch'ing Wu   121

29. The Mad Beggar: Chou Tien   125

30. The Old Man and the Kingmaker:
    Huang-shih Kung and Chang Liang   129

31. Master of Ghost Valley: Kuei-ku Tzu   133

32. Master of K'an-yu: Kuo P'u   136

33. The Reader of Dynastic Destiny:
    Lin Ling-su   140

V. ALCHEMISTS

34. The Master of Spirit Travel: Chang Po-tuan   147

35. The Father of T'ai-Chi Ch'uan:
    Chang San-feng   150

36. The Woman Who Could Turn Minerals into
    Gold: Cheng Wei's Wife   153

37. The Sage Who Embraced Simplicity:
    Ko Hung   156

38. The Poet Immortal: Pai Yü-ch'an   160

39. Lady of the Great Yin: T'ai-yin Nü   163

40. The Father of Immortal Alchemy:
    Wei Po-yang   166

Introduction

WHEN I WAS GROWING UP in Hong Kong, my grandmother told me many stories about the Taoist immortals. We'd sit cross-legged on her bed together and while she sewed, she would tell me how Iron Crutch Li (T'ieh-kuai Li) got his name, how Fan Li and Hsi Shih helped the king of Yüeh defeat the kingdom of Wu, and how Mah Ku saved the people of her town by imitating the crowing of roosters.

The immortals are very much a part of my culture. The Chinese people's belief in immortals goes back to the ancient times of prehistory and legend, centuries before Taoism became a philosophy and a spiritual tradition. Chinese children in traditional families grew up listening to stories of the immortals, and I was no exception. Even before I had heard of Taoism and practiced its teachings, I was familiar with the exploits of the immortals.

My grandmother was not the only person who told me these tales; there were also regular storytelling sessions on the radio. I remember one program especially well: it aired in the late afternoon, and it featured actors who not only had an endless repertoire of stories but could also impersonate the voices of women, men, and children. I looked forward to every show and rarely missed one. It was from these on-air storytellers that I learned about Lü Tung-pin's pillow and his dream, Chen Hsi-yi's game of chess with the Sung emperor, and Fei Chang-fang's friendship with the man in the gourd.

When I was a child, the stories of Taoist immortals were also dramatized in opera. Before Hong Kong became a bustling city crowded with skyscrapers and shopping centers, Chinese opera troupes performed frequently in the streets.

On the day before a performance, a street, usually one near a marketplace, would be closed. Workers would build the stage, set up rows of benches, and erect little tents where the performers could rest between acts. Large scaffolds decorated with flowers and banners would be placed around the stage and the seating area, and written on the banners were the names of the principal singers. Whenever a troupe visited my neighborhood, our entire household—my parents, my grandmother, myself, and the servants—would go to the performances. I still have vivid memories of those shows; they were the only occasions when I was allowed to stay up late. The operas didn't begin until dark, and, on a summer night in Hong Kong, that usually meant nine.

In Chinese opera, the performers were not only singers but also acrobats and martial artists. The stories of the immortals—Chang Tao-ling's battle with the lords of evil, Chu Yüan-chang's (the founder of the Ming dynasty) treacherous betrayal of his friends, Kiang Tzu-ya using his magic to defeat the evil emperor—came alive as the performers sang, whirled, sparred, and somersaulted around the stage.

Then, there are the legends as told by the professional storytellers in Banyan Tree Park. When I was younger, the park was located along a stretch of waterfront near a typhoon shelter. Every night the park, which consists of an area around a huge banyan tree, would be crowded with food vendors, gamblers, storytellers, acrobats, and martial artists displaying their skills. I distinctly remember one burly man walking around with a sign that read "Eagle claw expert—will accept challenges from any style." As a teenager, I was not allowed to go to the park alone. I was told there were pickpockets, kidnappers, and all sorts of mean people hanging out in that section of town at night. Only when my older cousins visited was I permitted to go to the park with them.

Banyan Tree Park is known as the Storytellers' Park for good reason: the finest professional storytellers in Hong Kong are found there. Every time I visited the park, I would make my way to the storytellers' stands, put a newspaper on the ground, and sit and listen to the tales of Chinese heroes and Taoist immortals. Each storyteller had his regular spot in the park, and at twilight each would walk to his designated place, carrying a thermos filled with tea and a small kerosene lamp. There each would sit on a folding chair and wait for his audience to gather. The best storytellers at Banyan Tree Park not only narrated, but also impersonated different voices, made sound effects, sang, and acted the roles of the characters in the stories. Each storyteller had his own repertoire, and the tales and the manner of telling them were all learned, memorized, and passed from one generation to another.

You can also read about Taoist immortals in the Taoist Canon, the collection of books that form the scriptures of Taoism. Personally, I've never been thrilled by the way the immortals are portrayed in these biographies. The entries read like articles from an encyclopedia and the characters appear dull and remote. After reading one, I always felt that I learned *about* the immortals rather than *from* them. On the other hand, in the operas, radio plays, and stories told by my grandmother and the Banyan Tree Park storytellers, the characters came alive. At the end of each story, I felt that I had not only met the immortals but had learned from them.

What are immortals? Were they mortals once, or have they been immortal since the beginning of time? The answer is a bit of both. In this book, you will find that some immortals were spirits of stars or animals (Tung-fang Shuo and Chang Kuo Lao); some were mortals who had done good deeds and were rewarded with immortality (the sisters in the story of Ko Hsüan); some entered the immortal realm by ingesting a magical pill (the Yellow Emperor, Huai-nan Tzu, Ko Hung, and Wei Po-yang); and still others attained immortality by cultivating body and mind (Ssu-ma Ch'eng-chen, Chen Hsi-yi, and Chang Po-tuan).

Taoist immortals can be divided into four classes according to their level of cultivation. At the lowest level are the human immortals. Human immortals are not very different from ordinary mortals except that they live long and healthy lives. In this book, Fan Li, Hsi Shih, and Kiang Tzu-ya are examples of human immortals.

Next come the earth immortals. These immortals live for an unusually long period of time in the mortal realm, far beyond the life span of ordinary people. In this book, Tso Chi, Fei Chang-fang, and Chang Chung are examples of earth immortals.

Above the earth immortals are the spirit immortals, who live forever in the celestial lands. Some, like the Yellow Emperor, Wei Po-yang, and Wen Shih, take their bodies with them when they enter the immortal realm. Others, like Pai Yü-ch'an, Kuo P'u, and Chang Po-tuan, leave their bodies behind when they liberate their spirits.

At the highest level are the celestial immortals. These immortals have been deified and given the titles of celestial lord, emperor, or empress. Some, like Lao Tzu and Chuang Tzu, are de facto deities because they are considered manifestations of the cosmic energy of the Tao. Others, like Lü Tung-pin and Ho Hsien-ku, were "promoted" to deity status because of the meritorious works they had done in the mortal and immortal realms.

Taoist immortals are as diverse as any group of people. Some were healers (Fei Chang-fang and Chang Tao-ling); some were teachers (Lü Tung-pin, Kuei-ku Tzu, T'ai-hsüan Nü, and T'ao Hung-ching); and some were social activists and politicians (Fan Li, Hsi Shih, and Chang Liang). Some cultivated the Tao by living in seclusion (Ko Hung, Ts'ao Kuo-chiu, and Chang San-feng), and others lived in society but shunned the values of the establishment (Chuang Tzu and Chou Tien). There were scientists (Cheng Wei's wife and Wei Po-yang); scholars (Ssu-ma Ch'eng-chen and Chang Po-tuan); poets (Han Hsiang and Lin Ling-su); military commanders (the Yellow Emperor, Chungli Ch'uan, and Kiang Tzu-ya); feng-shui masters (Kuo P'u and Ch'ing Wu); aristocrats (Huai-nan Tzu and Ts'ao Kuo-chiu); entertainers (Lan Ts'ai-ho and Tso Chi); householders (Ho Hsien-ku and T'ang Kuang-chen); and entrepreneurs (Fan Li and T'ai-yin Nü).

However, despite their diversity, the immortals all have these things in common: they were interested in the Tao at an early age; they shunned fame and fortune; and they lived simple and unencumbered lives. Some, following the example of Chuang Tzu, were never attracted to public life. Others, following the teachings of the *Tao-te-ching*, retired from public service after their work was done.

In the Taoist tradition, the stories of immortals are meant to teach as well as to entertain. For example, the stories of Fan Li and Hsi Shih, Chang Liang, Chou Tien, and Chang Chung warn us that power corrupts, and that even those with good intentions in the beginning (like Chu Yüan-chang and Liu Pang) can easily become murderous villains. In the story of the students of Kuei-ku Tzu, we learn the importance of knowing to retire at the appropriate time. The stories also promote virtues such as generosity (Ch'ing

Wu and Sun Chung), kindness (Ko Hsüan and the sisters), integrity and courage (Mah Ku), filial piety (Ho Hsien-ku and T'ang Kuang-chen), and dedication (Wen Shih).

Even the immortals themselves learned lessons in these tales. T'ao Hung-ching had to learn to value all sentient life (including worms and insects) before he could attain immortality; T'ieh-kuai Li was too vain and had to take on the appearance of an ugly cripple to learn humility before he could complete his training; and Lü Tung-pin had to be shocked by a nightmare before he would awaken from his illusions.

The immortals I have chosen to include in this book are the most well known and respected among the Chinese. Their names are household words, and their stories are told and retold throughout generations.

In telling these stories, I have tried to preserve the style of traditional Chinese storytelling. The immortals are listed in the category for which they are best known—sages, magicians, diviners, and alchemists. However, as you read the stories, you will notice that many immortals do not belong to one category exclusively. For example, Chen Hsi-yi, who is best known as a sage, was also a diviner, and T'ai-hsüan Nü, who is best known as a magician, was also an alchemist. The Eight Immortals, the most famous of the Taoist immortals, are included in a separate section and are listed in their order of seniority. As a group, the Eight Immortals represent the many facets of Taoist spirituality: teaching (Lü Tung-pin), alchemy (Chungli Ch'uan), female cultivation (Ho Hsien-ku), divination (Chang Kuo Lao), spirit travel (T'ieh-kuai Li), the hermit tradition (Ts'ao Kuo-chiu), an unencumbered lifestyle (Lan Ts'ai-ho), and love of the arts (Han Hsiang). No other immortals have inspired the cultural arts of China or fired the imagination of the Chinese people as much as the Eight Immortals.

Taoist immortals have been role models for the Chinese for centuries and have represented everything that we value as a culture. Now, as more non-Chinese are beginning to embrace Taoism as a spiritual tradition, the immortals have taken on an even more significant role: they have gone beyond being cultural symbols of the Chinese to become universal examples of spiritual attainment.

I thank the writers of the Chinese operas, the storytellers on the radio and at Banyan Tree Park, and, most of all, my grandmother for passing on to me one of the greatest treasures of Taoism. I hope that you will enjoy these stories of the immortals as much as I have.

PART ONE

The Eight Immortals

1
The Guest of
the Cavern
Lü Tung-pin

Lü Tung-pin's original name was Lü Yen. It is said that when Lü Yen was born, the sound of flutes and pipes was heard and a white crane came to sit by his mother's bed. The chamber was filled with fragrance, and multicolored clouds were seen hovering at the window.

Lü Yen's grandfather was a supervisor of rites and rituals, and his father was a secretary in the police department. Like the sons of many government officials, he aspired to follow in the footsteps of his father and grandfather. He studied the Confucian classics, wrote poetry, and practiced the martial arts. However, he was also interested in Taoism and admired the sages Chang Liang and Fan Li, who, after serving their country, had retired to cultivate the Tao.

When Lü Yen was twenty years old, he met a Taoist who told him, "You have the makings of an immortal and are destined to live in a thatched hut rather than a golden mansion. When you meet a man named Chungli Ch'uan, you should seize the opportunity."

The years passed. Lü Yen had taken the civil service examinations twice and failed each time. On his way to the capital for one last try, he stopped at an inn for the night. By now, Lü Yen's enthusiasm for a government career had diminished substantially. He sat at a table, ordered wine, and sighed as he drank. After a few mouthfuls of wine, he heard a voice behind him say, "No need to sigh and drink by yourself. Tell me what's on your mind."

Lü Yen turned and saw a man smiling at him. The stranger was dressed in a short tunic open down to his waist to reveal a tuft of hair on his chest. The legs of his pants were rolled up; he had straw sandals on his feet; his hair was tied into two knots on the sides of his head; and in his hand was a large fan.

Lü Yen was fascinated by the man. He walked over, sat down at the stranger's table, and told him of his disappointment at not being able to serve his country. At the end of his story, Yen added, "I am ready to leave the world of fame and fortune and devote my life to cultivating the Tao."

The strange man then said, "My name is Chungli Ch'uan. I am also called the Hermit of the Cloud Chamber. Would you like to follow me into the mountains and learn about the Tao?"

Lü Yen did not know what to do. On one hand, he wanted to abandon everything and follow Ch'uan into the mountains. On the other hand, he was still attached to social conventions and responsibilities. When Ch'uan saw the conflict within Lü Yen, he said, "Come, let us have dinner. You can let me know later."

After dinner, Lü Yen was still hesitant about following the strange man into the mountains. Ch'uan saw this and said, "I will not force you." He then gave Yen a pillow as a parting gift.

That night, Lü Yen slept with his head on the pillow and dreamed that he had passed the civil service examinations and had become a high-ranking official. He was appointed chief minister in the emperor's court; he married and had many children and grandchildren; and he was respected by all. Then the dream took an ugly turn. Lü Yen saw himself embroiled in court intrigues. Ministers jealous of Yen's relationship with the emperor framed him for treason, and his entire family was arrested. First, all his male children and grandchildren were executed. Then, his family shrine was destroyed. Finally, he was exiled to the frontier, where he died, far from his surviving relatives.

Lü Yen woke up from his nightmare trembling and covered with sweat. Quickly, he ran out of his room to look for Ch'uan, who was sitting at a table having his morning tea. When he saw Yen, he said, "In one night, you have lived through twenty years of your life."

"Then you knew about my dream?" asked Lü Yen.

The Taoist replied, "You achieved your goals in your dream, but you also lost everything. Gains and losses are illusions of the mortal realm. Only those who can see through illusions are capable of transcending them."

"Take me with you into the mountains," said Lü Yen. "From now on fame, riches, and social prestige are nothing to me."

Chungli Ch'uan congratulated him, "You have awakened from your illusions—this is your first step to cultivating the Tao. However, before I can teach you the arts of longevity and immortality, you need to strengthen your foundations. Right now, your body is weak and your mind is cluttered. When you have built the proper foundations, I will come back to teach you."

Lü Yen thanked Ch'uan and they parted. Yen walked out of the inn and told himself, "From now on, I am no longer Lü Yen the scholar. I will take the name Lü Tung-pin (guest of the cavern), for now I understand I am but a visitor in this realm learning how to return to my original home."

Lü Tung-pin built a thatched hut and settled in the Chung-nan Mountains. He emptied his mind, strengthened his body, and lived the simple life of a hermit.

One day, Chungli Ch'uan appeared at the door of Tung-pin's retreat and said, "I see that you have worked hard to cultivate your mind and body. Now you are ready to learn the Taoist arts. First, I'll teach you how to turn stones into gold."

Lü Tung-pin asked his teacher, "After the stones have been turned into gold, will they remain as gold forever?"

Ch'uan replied, "No. The gold nuggets will revert back to stones after three thousand years."

Tung-pin then said, "I would rather not learn a technique that could potentially delude and harm people."

Ch'uan sighed and admitted, "Your understanding of the Tao surpasses mine."

After Lü Tung-pin had completed his training with Chungli Ch'uan, the elder immortal said, "I must return to the celestial realm. If you wish, you can journey with me."

Tung-pin bowed to his teacher and said, "Our paths are different. You are meant to wander leisurely in the celestial

lands. As for me, I will not enter the highest realm of immortality until I have helped all sentient beings return to
the Tao."

Ch'uan bowed deeply to his former student and said,
"Your deeds on behalf of the Tao will be far greater than
mine." With that, he walked into a bank of fog and disappeared. Lü Tung-pin descended from his mountain retreat
and wandered around the countryside, teaching all those
who wanted to learn about the Tao.

LÜ YEN lived from the end of the T'ang dynasty (618–906 CE)
through the Five Dynasties (907–960 CE) and into the early part
of the Sung (960–1279 CE). He was the teacher of Wang Ch'ung-
yang, the founder of the Northern Complete Reality School; Liu
Hai-ch'an, the founder of the Southern Complete Reality School;
and Chen Hsi-yi, the founder of the Earlier Heaven Limitless
Way. His poetry and treatises on cultivating the Tao are collected
in the *Lü Tsu ch'üan-shu (The Complete Works of Patriarch Lü)*.

2

Hermit of the Cloud Chamber

Chungli Ch'uan

Chungli Ch'uan was the son of a high-ranking government official. His family had served the Han empire for several generations, and Ch'uan was expected to follow in the footsteps of his ancestors.

It was said that when Chungli Ch'uan was born, a dazzling light appeared outside his mother's chamber. The light was so bright the guards in the household fell on their knees and covered their eyes. Ch'uan's looks were extraordinary. He had a large forehead, long ears, and bright round eyes. His cheeks were rosy, his lips were the color of red cinnabar, and his arms were long and thick. After he tumbled out of his mother's womb, Ch'uan did not cry or fret. On the seventh day after he was born, he smiled, jumped to his feet, and surprised everyone by saying, "Today I'm going to the Purple Chamber of the immortals to play!"

Chungli Ch'uan grew up to be a strong and intelligent young man. The emperor was impressed with his demeanor and appointed him general.

Once, Ch'uan led a military excursion to the western borders of the Han empire, into a desert region called Turfan. His army was overcome by the fierce warriors of the desert, and, fleeing from his pursuers, Ch'uan was soon lost in a maze of canyons with steep walls. When night fell, he sat on a rock and pondered his fate.

"Am I destined to die here?" he asked himself.

"Not if you follow my advice," responded a voice in the darkness.

Chungli Ch'uan turned and saw a man dressed in rags and animal skins. Eagle and hawk feathers hung from his hair, and around his neck was a string of lion teeth. Ch'uan was at first apprehensive, but the man said, "General, I can take you to a place where you can be safe from your pursuers."

The stranger led Ch'uan through what seemed to be an endless labyrinth of deep valleys. Presently, they arrived at an oasis. The man stopped and said, "This is where the Celestial Lord of the East attained the Tao. You will be able to spend a night here in peace." Then he disappeared.

Chungli Ch'uan walked into the oasis and found a mansion. Not wanting to disturb its occupants, he stood at the entrance and waited. Soon a voice came from the courtyard: "That shaman must have led you here." The door opened, and the general saw an old man dressed in white deer hide standing in front of him. Before Ch'uan could greet him, the old man said loudly, "You must be Chungli Ch'uan, the general of the Han empire. You are welcome to stay here."

Chungli Ch'uan realized that the man was no ordinary mortal. He immediately fell to his knees and begged the old man to teach him the arts of immortality.

After three days, Ch'uan's host said to him, "I have taught you enough to get you started on the road to immortality. When the time comes, other teachers will appear and guide you further."

Thanking his teacher, Ch'uan left the mansion. At the mouth of the canyon, he turned to have a last look at the place that had changed his destiny. To his shock, both the mansion and the oasis had disappeared.

Chungli Ch'uan never returned to the capital. He traveled throughout the country and learned the arts of the Tao from hermits and wandering sages. Eventually, he mastered the arts of immortality and ascended to the celestial realm.

CHUNGLI CH'UAN lived during the Han dynasty (206 BCE– 219 CE) and was a general of the Han empire before he became a practitioner of the arts of immortality.

3

The Patron of Female Taoists

Ho Hsien-ku

In Kuangtung Province in southern China lived a well-to-do family by the name of Ho. This family had a daughter who was born with six golden hairs on her head.

When she was fourteen, Lady Ho dreamed that she met an immortal who told her, "If you eat the sands of the Cloud Mother River, your body will become light and you will live forever." Because the dream was so vivid, Lady Ho followed the instructions immediately.

"I wish to remain single and devote the rest of my life to cultivating the Tao," she told her parents. Her father was not pleased when he heard this. He had planned to marry her off to a rich man and relented only when her mother reminded him, "Do you remember that our daughter was born with six strands of golden hair? She's no ordinary woman and we should respect her wishes."

Lady Ho continued to live with her parents, but often she would disappear into the mountains to gather herbs and minerals. Her gait was so swift that she could leave at sunrise, travel for hundreds of miles, and return home at sunset with fruit for her mother.

After her parents passed away, Lady Ho retreated into the mountains and abstained from grains completely. In winter she could sleep on ice and not be chilled; in summer she was not bothered by the heat. Scholars who came to challenge her understanding of Taoism were silenced and awed by her knowledge and breadth of learning.

Lady Ho's reputation as an adept in the arts of longevity caught the attention of the T'ang empress.

"Find this Taoist woman and bring her back to the palace," the empress told her personal guards. To herself, she said, "If I can master the arts of immortality, I'll be able to sit on the throne and rule forever."

The guards found Lady Ho and related the empress's wishes to her. "The empress has heard of your abilities and desires to see an immortal," they said.

But Lady Ho knew what was in the empress's mind. "The arts of immortality are not meant to be abused by those who are selfish and power-hungry," she said to herself. So one night, when the company was just a few days' walk from the capital, she slipped away.

When the guards returned empty-handed, the empress flew into a rage and shouted, "You incompetent fools! Go and put up posters offering a large reward to anyone who can give me information of Lady Ho's whereabouts."

One time, the empress received reports of Lady Ho flying up to the sky on the outskirts of the capital. When the imperial guards arrived, the immortal was nowhere to be seen.

Another time, the empress was told that Lady Ho was sitting on a shrine together with the female immortal Mah Ku. But when the soldiers got there, Lady Ho could not be found.

Yet another time, Lady Ho was reported to be in a small town in Kuangtung. The local magistrate quickly sent a message to the capital, but by the time the empress's men arrived, Lady Ho had again disappeared.

Ho Hsien-ku lived during the T'ang dynasty (618–906 CE) and is regarded by many as the patron of female Taoist practitioners.

4

The Bat Spirit

Chang Kuo Lao

Chang Kuo was a master of magic and divination. Because he always appeared as an old man, he was called Chang Kuo Lao, meaning "Chang Kuo the Old Man."

Kuo had a white mule, a magical animal that could travel thousands of miles a day. When he did not need the mule, he would command the animal to step onto a piece of paper. The mule would be transformed into a picture, and Chang Kuo would fold up the paper and put it in a small box. When he needed the mule, he would unfold the paper, and the animal would reappear, ready for him to ride.

The T'ang emperor heard about Kuo's magical abilities

and asked the Taoist to become his adviser; Chang Kuo refused.

Later, Empress Wu tried to invite Kuo to serve her; he pretended to die. When the imperial messengers arrived at Kuo's home, they found his body lying in the courtyard covered with maggots. After the envoys had left to report the Taoist's death to the empress, Kuo got up and walked away.

Still another emperor tried to enlist Kuo's services. Knowing that it would be difficult to persuade the Taoist to serve in his court, the emperor asked Fei Wu, a friend of Kuo's, to be the emissary. When Fei Wu arrived with the emperor's message, Chang Kuo stopped his breath and "died." Wu fell to his knees, wept, and begged for forgiveness. Moved by his friend's sincerity, Kuo sat up. Fei Wu apologized for intruding and returned to the capital.

The emperor tried again to invite Chang Kuo to the palace. This time he sent his personal secretary, along with a letter promising the Taoist that he would not be pressed into service. This time Kuo agreed to meet the emperor.

He entertained the emperor with his magic and told him stories of life in the immortal realm, but he never talked about himself.

After a while, the emperor got curious about Chang Kuo's identity. He summoned his court diviner, a Buddhist named Yeh Fa-shan, and asked him, "What do you know about this man?"

Fa-shan replied, "My lord, I dare not disclose Chang Kuo's identity, for if I do, I'll die."

"I will personally guarantee you will not die," the emperor assured him.

Fa-shan then said, "If anything happens to me after I tell

you who Chang Kuo really is, you must take off your crown and your shoes and ask the lords of heaven to intervene and save me."

When the emperor agreed, Fa-shan said, "Chang Kuo was originally a bat spirit. He attained human form by absorbing the essences of the sun and the moon." The diviner tried to continue, but no words came from his mouth. Moments later, Fa-shan fell to the ground and died.

Shocked, the emperor immediately took off his crown and his shoes, went down on his knees, and begged the lords of heaven to save his diviner.

Chang Kuo appeared and said, "Sire, this man knew the consequences when he revealed the secrets of heaven."

The emperor begged, "It was my fault that he died. Let me take the punishment."

Moved by the emperor's integrity, Chang Kuo allowed, "I will see what I can do." He threw some water on Fashan's body, and the diviner immediately sat up.

Not long after this incident, Chang Kuo asked for permission to leave the palace. The emperor sent him off with gifts of cloth and gold and two assistants. Kuo declined the cloth and gold but took the assistants. At the foot of Mount Heng, Kuo sent one of the assistants home and took the other with him into the mountains.

A year later, the emperor tried to invite Chang Kuo back to the palace. However, when the imperial messenger arrived at Kuo's retreat, the master stopped his breath and died. Weeping, Kuo's assistant lit the funeral candles and put his master's body in a coffin.

After the emissary had gone, the lid of the casket flew open. The assistant peeked in and, to his shock, found that Kuo's body had disappeared.

When news of Chang Kuo's "disappearance" reached

the capital, the emperor ordered a shrine to be built on Mount Heng to honor the bat-spirit immortal.

CHANG KUO LAO lived during the T'ang dynasty (618–906 CE). He wrote a treatise on astrology titled *Chang Kuo Lao hsing-tsung (Chang Kuo Lao's Astrological System)*. This system of celestial divination is still used widely by Chinese seers today.

5

The Immortal with the Iron Crutch

T'ieh-kuai Li

T'ieh-kuai means "Iron Crutch," and Li got this nickname in an extraordinary way. He was an adept in the arts of longevity and spirit travel; it is said he learned them directly from Lao Tzu himself. Tall, handsome, and charismatic, Li was proud of his good looks and youthful vitality, which he maintained as a result of his practice.

One day, Li was invited to a gathering of immortals on Mount Hua. Before he sent out his spirit, he told his servant, "I will be leaving my body for seven days. Make sure that nothing happens to it while my spirit is gone. If I don't wake up after sunset on the seventh day, you can burn my body, gather your belongings, and go home." With that, he closed his eyes, laid down, and sent his spirit to Mount Hua.

Six days passed, and Li had not returned. On the morning of the seventh day, the servant received a message from his brother, telling him that their mother was severely ill and would die soon. Li's servant was caught in a dilemma. "I need to go home and see my mother before she dies," he said to himself. "But the master told me to watch over his body for seven days." He fretted for a long time and then decided, "Today is the seventh day and my master has not returned. It probably won't matter whether I burn the body now or wait till after sunset."

The servant built a pyre, placed Li's body on it, and set the wood on fire. After making sure that the body was burned to ashes, he packed his belongings and went home.

That evening at sunset, Li's spirit returned. When he saw the funeral pyre outside his house, he sighed and said, "It is the will of heaven."

At that time, Li had not attained immortality and still needed a human shell to complete his cultivation. Fluttering around the town, his spirit found a beggar who had just died. The beggar was crippled and ugly, and, under normal circumstances, Li would have been too vain to choose so grotesque a shell. But he was desperate. If his spirit did not enter a body soon, he would lose his chance to complete his cultivation. So Li's spirit hastily entered the body of the crippled beggar. From that time on, Li appeared as a crippled beggar leaning on an iron crutch.

Not much is known about T'IEH-KUAI LI except that he lived during the T'ang dynasty (618–906 CE).

6
A Faithful Nephew
Han Hsiang

Han Hsiang was the nephew of the great scholar Han Yü. Although learned in the classics and talented at poetry and music, Hsiang had no intentions of entering the government.

While most young men of his age were busy studying for the civil service examinations, Han Hsiang was wandering around the mountains playing his flute and writing poetry. One time, while climbing up Mount Hua, Hsiang met the immortal Lü Tung-pin. Knowing the young poet was destined to become an immortal, Tung-pin taught Hsiang the arts of longevity and magic.

In the capital, Hsiang's uncle Han Yü was worried over his nephew's lack of interest in the government. One day, he called Hsiang to him and said, "It is your duty to use your talent to serve the emperor. You should stop drifting around and start preparing for the imperial examinations."

Hsiang replied, "Our paths are different. You are destined to be famous in the realm of mortals and I am meant to escape the dust of the world." He waved his hand and a flask of wine and two cups appeared on the table.

"Let us drink together, for this is my last day in the capital," Hsiang told his uncle. "Beware of those in power. If we meet again, it will be on a snowy night at the frontier."

At that time, Han Yü did not understand his nephew's words.

Several days after Hsiang had left the capital, Han Yü was arrested for criticizing the emperor's decision to enshrine Buddhist relics in the capital. Despite pleas from several influential ministers, the emperor had Yü demoted. The foremost scholar of the imperial academy was ordered to serve as a supervisor of courier service in a small frontier town.

Sadly, Han Yü made his way to the border. At Lan Pass, Yü was caught in a snowstorm. Night was falling and there was no shelter in sight. Just as he was giving up hope, Han Yü saw someone walking toward him. To his surprise, it was his nephew.

Han Hsiang approached his uncle and said, "Do you remember the conversation we had on my last night in the capital?"

Yü nodded. "I should have taken your advice and not criticized the emperor's actions. But what has happened cannot be undone."

Hsiang led Yü to an inn and ordered wine, and uncle and nephew talked long into the night. The next morning, as

Han Yü got ready to leave, Hsiang urged, "Uncle, do not despair. You will suffer hardships, but you will eventually be welcomed back to the capital."

Han Yü embraced his nephew and asked, "Will we meet again?"

Hsiang replied, "That I do not know."

Han Yü spent several years at the frontier. Then, as Han Hsiang had predicted, an imperial messenger arrived to invite Yü back to the capital. "The charges against you have been dropped," said the emissary. "You are to return and be promoted."

Han Yü returned to the capital to serve his emperor. He would eventually become one of the greatest poets, essayists, and scholars of China. Han Hsiang attained immortality, sought out his old friend Lü Tung-pin, and joined the company of the Eight Immortals.

HAN HSIANG lived during the T'ang dynasty (618–906 CE). His uncle, Han Yü, was one of the Eight Great Scholars of the T'ang and Sung dynasties.

7

The Wandering Minstrel

Lan T'sai-ho

No one knows where Lan Ts'ai-ho came from. The legends say that he was always dressed in colorful rags, had flowers in his hair, and carried a three-foot-long branch that he used as a walking stick. Sometimes he would dress as a male and sometimes as a female. He wore only one shoe; the other foot was always bare. In summer he would stuff cotton and wool into his clothing; in winter he would lie naked on the ice and blow hot breath from his mouth.

Ts'ai-ho had no home. He wandered around the towns and villages entertaining people and never stayed in one place for more than a month. His favorite haunts were restaurants and wine shops, where he would drink and entertain the patrons with songs about life in the immortal lands. But T'sai-ho's favorite audiences were the children and the elderly who gathered at the street corners to hear him sing.

Whenever Ts'ai-ho was given coins for his performance, he would tie them to a string and drag them behind him as he walked. If he lost his money, he was not concerned. If he had money left after paying for his food and drinks, he would give it to the poor.

One day, while eating and drinking on the terrace of a restaurant, Lan Ts'ai-ho heard the music of reeds and pipes. When a crane flew down from the sky and landed on his table, he knew it was time for him to leave for the immortal realm. He jumped onto the crane's back, threw his shoe and sash on the ground, and flew up to the sky. When the people in the street tried to pick up his belongings, both the shoe and the sash vanished.

While wandering around in the immortal lands, Lan Ts'ai-ho met Lü Tung-pin and Chungli Ch'uan. Taken by Ts'ai-ho's carefree manner and beautiful voice, the two elder immortals invited the youth to travel with them to visit the famous mountains and lakes of the celestial realm.

LAN TS'AI-HO lived during the Five Dynasties (907–960 CE). Not much is known about him except that he was a street entertainer and was famous for his beautiful singing voice.

8

The Hermit
Aristocrat

Ts'ao Kuo-chiu

Ts'ao was a brother of the queen mother and the *kuo-chiu*
(maternal uncle) of the emperor. However, despite being
born into nobility, he was not interested in politics and
power. His younger brother, on the other hand, was ruthless and cruel and used his royal connections to obtain land,
jewels, and even other men's wives.

When Ts'ao failed to steer his brother away from his un-
ethical ways, he said to himself, "There is nothing left for
me to do in the palace." He left the capital, went into the
woods, and devoted his life to cultivating the Tao.

One day, the immortals Lü Tung-pin and Chungli Ch'uan happened to walk by Ts'ao's retreat.

Lü Tung-pin called out, "I've heard that you had given up the life of a prince to cultivate the Tao. Tell me, where's the Tao that you are cultivating?"

Ts'ao pointed to the sky.

Immortal Lü then said, "And where's heaven?"

Ts'ao pointed to his heart.

Immortal Chungli Ch'uan clapped his hands and exclaimed, "Well said. The way of the Tao is the way of heaven and the way of heaven is in your heart. You have seen your original nature."

The three men laughed together. Lü Tung-pin and Chungli Ch'uan then invited Ts'ao to travel with them to the immortal realm.

TS'AO KUO-CHIU lived during the early part of the Sung dynasty (960–1279 CE). Not much is known about him except that he shunned nobility and devoted his life to studying the Tao.

PART TWO

Sages

陳希夷

9

The Father of Ch'i-Kung

Chen Hsi-yi

Chen Hsi-yi was born into a well-to-do family as Chen Tuan. He did not speak until he was five, but once he began, he could read and write and quote the Confucian and Taoist classics from memory. By fifteen he had also mastered the arts of divination, medicine, and astronomy.

When Chen Tuan's parents died, he said to his relatives, "What I learned in the past was book knowledge. From now on, I will seek out living teachers to show me how to cultivate the Tao." So Tuan sold all his possessions, gave the money to the poor, and left his home.

His decision to devote his life to cultivating the Tao was admired by scholars, intellectuals, and would-be Taoist practitioners alike. Many approached him, asking to be accepted as students. However, Tuan was not interested in their company. He knew that these people were not really interested in cultivating the Tao; they only wanted to be recognized as "sages" so they could be appointed to government positions.

The T'ang emperor invited Chen Tuan to the palace. When Tuan arrived at court, he did not prostrate himself before the throne. Instead, he merely bowed. The imperial officials were shocked by this behavior, but Chen Tuan's actions made the emperor respect him even more.

"I will be honored if you will become my adviser," the emperor said to Chen Tuan.

Tuan thanked the emperor, but court life did not appeal to him. So as not to offend the emperor, he wrote a poem explaining why he could not stay.

For the next twenty years, Chen Tuan lived in the Wutang Mountains, devoting his time to studying and practicing the arts of longevity. Later, he moved to Mount Hua, where he met the immortal Lü Tung-pin and learned the technique of spirit travel.

Chen Tuan was fond of practicing a form of ch'i-kung called "sleeping meditation." Often, he would "sleep" for days and even months. Once, a woodcutter looked inside the cave where Chen Tuan was meditating and thought he saw a corpse. When the woodcutter went in to have a closer look at the dead man, Chen Tuan suddenly sat up and said, "I was having such a good sleep. Why did you disturb me?" The woodcutter turned and ran down the slope.

Once, Chen Tuan ran into a crowd of peasants fleeing from a burning village. At that time, the T'ang dynasty had fallen and the countryside was devastated by civil war. Among the refugees was a woman carrying a basket, and inside the basket were two tiny infants. Chen Tuan heard one of the peasants say, "Where can we find an emperor who will bring peace to the land?" He pointed to the woman with the children and said, "There are your two emperors." These children were Chao Kang-yin, who would become the first emperor of the Sung dynasty, and his younger brother, who would succeed him as the second emperor.

Another time, Chen Tuan saw three men walking into an inn. The men sat down at a table and ordered wine. Approaching the eldest of the group, Chen Tuan said, "You are only a subordinate star in the presence of the Great North Star. You can never hope to be your companions' equal." It turned out that the two young men were Chao Kang-yin and his brother, the future emperors; the older man was destined to become only a minor noble.

When Chao Kang-yin became emperor, he remembered Chen Tuan's predictions and decided to ask the sage to be his adviser. When Tuan told the emperor that he preferred the company of the clouds around Mount Hua to that of people, Chao Kang-yin sighed and thought to himself, "This man has shaken off the dust of the world. I don't think I'll ever be able to keep him in the palace." Aloud, he said to Chen Tuan, "I will respect your wishes. But, let us remain friends. Some day, when the country is prosperous and peaceful again, I would like to learn more about the Tao." So Chen Tuan returned to his retreat on Mount Hua.

During the early years of Chao Kang-yin's reign, the country was still ravaged by rebels and bandits. The emperor looked at the maps of his kingdom and noticed that Mount Hua would be a perfect place to build a garrison.

However, the mountain was sacred to the Taoists; it was also where Chen Tuan had built his hermitage. The Sung emperor decided to pay the sage a visit.

As the emperor approached Tuan's retreat, the sage was already standing in front of his door waiting. Before Chao Kang-yin could bring up the subject of building a garrison, Chen Tuan said, "Let's play a game of chess. If you win, you can do whatever you want on the mountain. However, if I win, you and your descendants must promise never to station troops on Mount Hua."

The emperor agreed. "I'm a good player," he thought. "I should have a good chance of winning."

Chen Tuan was not only a good player, but he was adept at divination. The sage foresaw the emperor's every move and won the game.

When Tuan told him how he had won the game, Chao Kang-yin laughed and said, "Your wisdom is mysterious and your abilities are rare. I will honor you with the name Chen Hsi-yi." (*Hsi* means "rare" and *yi* means "mysterious.") From that time on, Chen Tuan was known by his new name.

The emperor left Mount Hua and, true to his promise, decreed that no garrisons were to be built on the mountain.

Chao Kang-yin was succeeded by his brother, who was crowned as Sung T'ai-tsung. T'ai-tsung also respected Chen Hsi-yi. He invited the sage to his palace and asked for advice on naming a successor.

"I would like you to see my son Chen-tsung and tell me if he would make a good ruler," the emperor said.

The sage replied, "I don't need to see your son to know that he will be a good emperor. On my way here, I looked at the faces of his guards and advisers and saw that these men are destined to become great generals and ministers."

Sung T'ai-tsung heeded Chen Hsi-yi's words and named Chen-tsung as his heir.

One summer, on the fifteenth day of the seventh month, Chen Hsi-yi said to his students, "It is time for me to journey to Mount Omei in the west." His students understood that their teacher meant it was time for him to leave the earthly realm, so they purified the room with incense and lit two tall candles. Hsi-yi sat on his bed in meditation posture, placed his palm on top of his head, and sent his spirit to the immortal realm. At that time, he was 118 years old.

CHEN HSI-YI lived from the end of the T'ang dynasty (618–906 CE), through the era of the Five Dynasties (907–960 CE), and into the early part of the Sung (960–1279 CE). He is acknowledged as the father of modern ch'i-kung and wrote important treatises on Taoist cosmology, divination, meditation, and calisthenics. He was the founding patriarch of the School of Taoism known as the Earlier Heaven Limitless Way.

10
Satirist of the High and Mighty

Chuang Tzu

Chuang Tzu was born Chuang Chou. He lived in the county of Mong in the kingdom of Ch'u and, for a brief period, held a minor post in the county government.

Although knowledgeable in the arts and sciences, Chuang Chou was not interested in pursuing a career as a statesman or a teacher. He did what he liked; ignored the social conventions of his time; and made fun of politicians, intellectuals, and businesspeople alike. No one, not even high-ranking officials, escaped Chou's satirical eye and sharp tongue.

Once, a friend came to visit Chuang Chou and found him asleep and snoring in the middle of the day. The friend nudged him gently and said, "It's well past noon. Everyone in town is out and about."

Chou sat up and murmured, "I dreamed that I was a butterfly fluttering among the flowers. Was I a man dreaming that I was a butterfly? Or am I a butterfly now dreaming that I am a man?"

The friend shook his head and went away.

Another time, the king of Ch'u, who admired Chuang Chou's learning, sent a messenger to ask Chou to be his adviser. When the messenger arrived at Chou's home with gifts of gold and cloth, Chou already knew what was in the king's mind. He said to the emissary, "I've heard that a giant tortoise that had died three thousand years ago has been decorated with jewels and is being displayed in a shrine. If you were the tortoise, would you rather be dead and decked out in jewels or wag your tail and wallow in the mud?"

Without hesitation, the messenger replied, "Of course, I would rather wag my tail and wallow in the mud."

Chuang Chou then said, "Tell the king that I too would prefer to wag my tail and roll around in the mud."

The king sent a second messenger to persuade Chuang Chou to serve him, but before the emissary could manage a word of greeting, Chou took him by the sleeve and led him to the king's stockyards. Inside a pen was a prize ox being fed with hay and grain of the highest quality. Pointing to the animal, Chuang Chou said to the king's messenger, "Look at this ox. He's being given the best foods, but he doesn't know that he'll be sacrificed at the autumn festival. When the butcher comes, he'll beg for the chance to pull a farmer's plough."

When the king learned of Chuang Chou's remarks, he said, "This man values his personal freedom more than anything else. I will not bother him again."

CHUANG TZU lived during the latter part of the Chou dynasty (1122–221 BCE) in the feudal state of Ch'u. He is reputed to be the primary author of the Taoist classic *Chuang Tzu*.

11

The Minister and the Courtesan

Fan Li and Hsi Shih

Fan Li was the chief adviser to Yu Chien, the lord of the kingdom of Yüeh. Yu Chien was a proud and willful ruler. Against his better judgment and his ministers' advice, he challenged the lord of Wu in battle and lost. Chien was taken prisoner and his kingdom made into a vassal state.

Fu Ts'o, the lord of the kingdom of Wu, was a cold and calculating man who distrusted even his closest advisers. Ts'o had inherited a strong and prosperous kingdom from

No illustration showing Hsi Shih could be found.

his father and had begun a campaign of conquest as soon as
he ascended the throne. Foremost in his mind had been
to incorporate the rich and fertile lands of Yüeh into his
kingdom.

Now that he had conquered Yüeh, Fu Ts'o wanted its
lord to become a willing vassal. First, he put Yu Chien in a
guarded but comfortable house. Then, he gave Chien servants and female companions, hoping that with time, Yu
Chien would voluntarily give up his kingdom and stay in
Wu. Indeed, if not for Fan Li, Chien would have become a
permanent "guest" under Fu Ts'o's watchful eye.

When Yu Chien was taken to Wu as a hostage, Fan Li
voluntarily followed his lord into captivity. Fu Ts'o could
hardly hide his delight at this choice. Fan Li was the most
able of Chien's ministers; it would be better to have him in
Wu where he could be watched, than back in Yüeh plotting
to free his master.

After several months of being treated as an honored
guest, Yu Chien forgot the humiliation of defeat and capture and began to entertain the prospect of becoming a citizen of Wu. When Fan Li saw this, he said to his lord, "Your
duty is to return to your homeland and free your kingdom,
not to sink into revelry and betray your people."

From that time on, lord and minister began to plot their
return to Yüeh. First, Yu Chien kept up the appearance of
delighting in fine foods, wine, and beautiful women. During the day, he drank and sang and cavorted with the courtesans. At night, however, he lay on a bed of straw and
sipped a bitter liquid from a gourd to remind himself of the
bitterness of captivity and the loss of his homeland.

While Yu Chien pretended to fall into the king of Wu's
trap, Fan Li began to gather information about Ts'o's hab-
its, and soon discovered that he had a weakness for women.

Fan Li's chance to use this knowledge came when Fu Ts'o ordered the vassal state of Yüeh to send him its most beautiful women as tribute. Fan Li got himself appointed as the recruiter of courtesans, arguing that as a native of Yüeh and a former minister, he knew where to find the best candidates.

Fan Li returned to Yüeh and set up a recruiting station in the capital. One day, a beautiful and stately woman walked into the tent. Surprised that a woman with such dignity would volunteer to become a courtesan, he asked for her name and said, "Why do you wish to serve a tyrant who has enslaved our country?"

"My name is Hsi Shih," the woman replied, "and I serve only the lord of Yüeh." When Hsi Shih explained that by being a courtesan, she could perhaps help Yu Chien return to his kingdom, Fan Li said, "I have finally met a kindred spirit in whom I can confide." Hsi Shih and Fan Li talked long into the night and came up with a plan to rescue Yu Chien and defeat Fu Ts'o.

Fan Li took Hsi Shih to Wu and presented her to Fu T'so along with the other courtesans. The king was so taken with Hsi Shih's beauty and intelligence that he made her his principal courtesan at their first meeting.

After Hsi Shih's arrival at the Wu court, Fu Ts'o began to spend more time with her and less time on the affairs of his kingdom. Hsi Shih played on his suspicious nature by spreading rumors about his ministers plotting to overthrow him. As a result of this, several of Wu's most able generals and ministers were executed for treason. She also persuaded Ts'o to tell her the locations of Wu's garrisons, as well as the strengths and weaknesses of each commander. Yu Chien and Fan Li soon had all the information they needed to defeat the kingdom of Wu.

One last task was left for Hsi Shih, and this was to persuade Fu Ts'o to let Yu Chien return to Yüeh. One day, when Ts'o was in a particularly receptive mood, Hsi Shih casually commented, "Yu Chien has become a womanizer and a drunk. He won't be a threat to your kingdom anymore. Why don't you send him home and save yourself the expense of keeping him here?" Fu Ts'o agreed and, against the advice of his ministers, released Yu Chien.

Once Yu Chien returned to his kingdom, he and Fan Li prepared to invade Wu. With the information provided by Hsi Shih, Yu Chien's defeat of Wu was sure and swift.

After conquering Fu Ts'o, Yu Chien called his advisers together and rewarded them with rich gifts. To Fan Li, he said, "I am especially grateful to you and Hsi Shih. I want you to be my chief minister. You and Hsi Shih can have all the land and gold you'll ever want."

Fan Li declined the offer politely and said, "Our most dangerous enemy has been removed; the country is prosperous; and you are a wise king. You will be a good ruler with or without me. Besides, Hsi Shih and I have always wanted to visit the famous mountains and rivers of the south."

Yu Chien was flattered by Fan Li's remarks. "You have my permission to leave," he said. "However, if I need you, I'll summon you back to the capital."

That night, Fan Li and Hsi Shih gathered their belongings into a boat and sailed south.

"Why did you decline the king's offer?" Hsi Shih asked Fan Li.

He replied, "Yu Chien the victorious conqueror is not the same man as Yu Chien the prisoner. Chien will befriend you when he needs your help. However, once he has attained his objective, he'll consider you a threat. He may be generous now, but in a few years there will be a purge. I'd rather leave freely than be forced to flee as a fugitive."

Fan Li and Hsi Shih hid their identities and traveled throughout southern China before they settled in a small town along the coast. There, Fan Li became a successful businessman, and although the couple accumulated a large fortune, they never displayed their wealth and never talked about their past. Not even their closest friends knew that Hsi Shih and Fan Li were the masterminds behind Yüeh's conquest of Wu.

FAN LI and HSI SHIH lived in the latter part of the Chou dynasty (1122–221 BCE). Fan Li was a minister in the state of Yüeh during a time when the feudal states of the Chou empire had become semiautonomous kingdoms. He is also revered as the patron of entrepreneurs in southern China.

12
The Yellow Emperor

Huang Ti

Huang Ti was the chieftain of a small tribe. Because bears roamed the region where his tribe had settled, he took the name Hsiung, which means "bear."

Hsiung was respected not only by his own tribe but by all those that settled along the Yellow River. Thus, when the tribes' camping grounds were attacked by bandits, he was asked to lead a group of warriors against the raiders.

The bandit leader, Chi Yu, was aggressive in battle and

Huang Ti (right) and Kuang-ch'en Tzu.

uncanny in strategy. Moreover, he had the help of evil shamans who could command fog and mist and summon rain
and snow.

After one especially ferocious battle, Chi Yu was cornered
and was about to be captured by Hsiung, when a fog suddenly descended on the valley. Chi Yu escaped, and Hsiung
and his warriors were trapped in a maze of canyons with
steep walls. For days, they wandered through the deep valleys, lost and disoriented.

Soon the warriors began to whisper among themselves,
"We have only one day of food and water left. If we don't
get out of these valleys soon, we will die."

Hsiung overheard them and said, "Stay calm. I will ask
the spirit guardians of this place to help us." He knelt
down, touched the ground with his head, and chanted a
prayer. Moments later, a shaft of light appeared through the
fog, and a female voice said, "Hsiung the Bear, you are
destined to unite the tribes and be their king. The Empress
of Heaven has sent me with these gifts for you."

When Hsiung looked up, he found that the fog had disappeared, and a woman wearing a robe of nine colors was
standing before him.

"I am the Lady of the Nine Heavens," the woman said,
"and here are the gifts from the Empress of Heaven."

The Lady first handed Hsiung a bowl containing a lodestone. She said, "This stone always points to the south.
With it, you will always be able to find your way in the fog."

Then she handed him two books and said, "The first
book will show you how to predict the movements of
your enemy. The other one will teach you how to defeat
Chi Yu."

Finally, the Lady gave Hsiung several objects of power

that included talismanic flags, eagle feathers, and two magical swords.

Hsiung studied the books of divination and military strategy and engaged Chi Yu again. This time, when Chi Yu's shamans conjured up a fog, Hsiung was not disoriented. Using the lodestone, he found his way to the enemy camp, attacked it, and captured the bandit leader.

After Chi Yu's defeat, the chieftains unanimously asked Hsiung to be their ruler. Hsiung was crowned king and given the name Huang Ti (Yellow Emperor).

Huang Ti labored for many years to bring peace and prosperity to his people. One summer, when he toured his kingdom and found that the land was fertile and the people contented, he said to himself, "I will now have time to learn about the Tao." Hearing that a sage named Kuang-ch'eng Tzu was living in a cave in the Hsiung-tung Mountains, Huang Ti decided to travel there to seek advice.

Upon finding the sage, Huang Ti bowed low and requested, "Teach me about the Tao."

Kuang-ch'eng Tzu replied, "After you became king, rain fell before the clouds became ominous; trees shed their leaves with the first wind from the north; and the light of the sun and moon shone on both grassland and desert. This is all I have to say about the Tao."

Huang Ti returned to his palace and pondered on the sage's words. "When things follow the natural way of the Tao, they are renewed," he said to himself. "However, after nineteen years of working for the welfare of my people I feel old and weak instead. I must be doing something wrong."

Three months later, Huang Ti returned to the mountains to see Kuang-ch'eng Tzu. When the sage saw the king, he asked, "Why did you return?"

Huang Ti replied, "Please teach me how to cultivate myself so that I can be renewed by the seasons and live as long as the sky and the earth."

Kuang-ch'eng Tzu said, "The Tao is intangible and formless. You cannot hear it or see it. However, if you focus your spirit, it will emerge within you. Empty your heart and still your mind. Preserve your generative energy and do not strain your body. Follow these teachings and you will live a long life."

When he returned to his palace, Huang Ti built a retreat. He distanced himself from the affairs of his kingdom and tried to live according to the teachings of Kuang-ch'eng Tzu. However, after three months of seclusion, not only was he unable to renew himself, but he got weaker by the day.

The king summoned his minister Li Wu and said irritably, "I have followed the teachings of the sage diligently. My health should be improving, not deteriorating!"

The minister said, "Sire, you are forcing things and not doing what is natural for you. You are a king, and it would be unnatural if you stopped ruling the country."

Huang Ti suddenly realized his mistake. He said to Li Wu, "You are right. Before, I was too involved with governing the country and forgot to cultivate myself. Now, I am too intent on cultivating myself and have neglected my duties as king."

From that time on, Huang Ti found a balance between practicing the arts of longevity and fulfilling his duties as a ruler.

After nine years, he finally succeeded in making the pill of immortality. The king made a tour of his country and, finding it peaceful and prosperous, knew that his work was done. He appointed a successor and, on a clear day, ingested the pill and rode off to the celestial realm on the back of a dragon.

HUANG TI, or the Yellow Emperor, lived in the legendary times of ancient China before written history. He is regarded as the wisest of all Chinese rulers and is credited with uniting the tribes into a nation, building the first cities, and giving China a written language and a numerical system.

13
The Old One
Lao Tzu

Lao Tzu's name was originally Li Erh. The legends say that on the night he was conceived, his mother saw an infant wrapped by the sun, moon, and clouds. On the morning of his birth, three suns rose from the east, and after he suckled, magic water came out of the mouths of nine dragons.

Li Erh was an extraordinary child. At three, his body radiated a golden glow. At five, he gazed at the sun and smiled and looked at the moon and sighed. At seven, he learned to swallow the rays of the sun, moon, and stars.

Not interested in becoming a statesman, Li Erh did not seek employment in the courts of the feudal states. Instead, he was content to work in the imperial library, where he could read and study the ancient rites and rituals.

One time, a young scholar named Kung Chung-ni came to the library to ask Li Erh about an obscure ritual. (Kung Chung-ni would later be known as Kung Tzu, or Confucius.) After answering the young man's questions, Li Erh told him, "You need to file down your sharpness and put away your sword of ambition. The great sage often appears dull and dim-witted, and those with true learning do not display their knowledge."

Years later, Chung-ni would recall this meeting and say, "Birds soar above the earth; fishes swim to the depths of the oceans; and tigers run the great expanse of the plains. But who can predict the behavior of dragons? Sometimes they fly among the clouds and sometimes they tunnel beneath the earth. Lao Tzu [the Old One] must have been a dragon. You could catch a glimpse of his wisdom, but if you tried to grasp it, it was gone."

Lao Tzu retired from the civil service not long after Chung-ni's visit. He traveled west and, at a border town near Han Ku Pass, dictated a treatise on the Tao and virtue to a man named Wen Shih. This book became known as the *Tao-te-ching*.

It was said that Lao Tzu continued to travel west after leaving Han Ku Pass. Eventually, he climbed up Mount K'un Lun and entered the immortal lands.

LAO TZU lived during the latter part of the Chou dynasty (1122–221 BCE) in the feudal state of Ch'u. He is regarded as the founder of the philosophy of Taoism and the author of the Taoist classic, the *Tao-te-ching*.

14
A Prince among Taoists
Liu An

Liu An was the grandson of the founder of the Han dynasty and held the title Prince of Huai-nan. As a youth, when his brothers and friends were attracted to hunting, archery, and chariot racing, Liu An preferred to play the zither, write poetry, and study the Taoist arts of longevity. When he succeeded his father as the lord of Huai-nan, he frequently invited scholars, sages, diviners, and alchemists to his court so that he could learn from them.

Liu An (left) with his teacher.

One day, eight old men appeared at the gates of Liu An's palace asking for an audience. The guards looked at them and said, "If you want to see our lord, you'd better have something to offer him. There are three things that our lord is especially interested in. First, he wants to learn the arts of longevity and immortality. Second, he wants to meet scholars of renown. Third, he wants to recruit retainers who are experts in the martial arts. You are all old and weak. What can you offer our lord?"

When the old men heard this challenge, they laughed and replied, "We have heard that the Prince of Huai-nan is a generous man and does not judge people by appearances. However, if you think that your master will only receive those who are young and able, then we will be glad to oblige him." Immediately the eight old men were transformed into youths.

The guards dropped to their knees, begged for forgiveness, and ran to inform their master that eight immortals had arrived. Liu An quickly went out to greet the visitors, who by then had resumed their appearance as old men. The prince knelt down, bowed to the men, and said, "It is an honor for me to receive such distinguished guests."

That night, Liu An prepared a feast to honor the eight Taoists. During the dinner, one of the old men stood up and said to the prince, "We see that you are sincere in your pursuit of the Tao. Each of us has a specialty that he can teach you. One of us can command the elements, make rain, and change the course of rivers. Another can move mountains, tame wild beasts, and summon spirits and ghosts. Another can hide the movement of armies and make them appear at different places at the same time. Another cannot be harmed by fire, water, or weapons. Another can create and craft anything he wants—animals, plants, or inanimate objects. Another can see impending disasters and is skilled in the arts of longevity and immortality. Another can transform dirt into gold and lead into silver. Still another can fly in the sky and tunnel beneath the earth. Of these skills, which would you like to learn?"

An replied, "All I wish is to be able to predict catastrophes and live a happy and long life."

Liu An spent nine years learning from the old men and eventually succeeded in making the pill of immortality. However, on the day that he completed his apprenticeship, his son was killed accidentally by one of the emperor's secretaries during a sword-fighting practice session. Fearing that the lord of Huai-nan would sentence him to death, the secretary told the emperor that Liu An was plotting a rebellion.

The evening before the emperor issued an order to arrest Liu An, the old men said to the prince, "You should leave the palace immediately. This is a warning from heaven. If you tarry, you'll be captured and executed."

Liu An heeded the advice of his teachers immediately. He went to his laboratory, took a pill from the cauldron, and swallowed it. In his hurry to leave the palace, An knocked the cauldron onto its side and scattered the remaining little red pills over the floor. Before the pills could be picked up by the servants, they were eaten by the cats and dogs in the household.

When the emperor's soldiers arrived at Liu An's palace, he was nowhere to be found. The officer questioned the townspeople, who told him, "We saw the lord of Huai-nan floating up to the sky with cats and dogs flying up behind him."

LIU AN, also known as Huai-nan Tzu, lived during the early part of the Han dynasty (206 BCE–219 CE). His court was a haven for Taoist alchemists, diviners, and magicians. He is reputed to have recorded and collected the teachings of his Taoist retainers into a classic titled *Huai-nan Tzu*.

15
The Hermit of Mount T'ien-tai

Ssu-ma Ch'eng-chen

Ssu-ma Ch'eng-chen learned the arts of the Tao from a hermit. After he completed his apprenticeship, Ch'eng-chen traveled throughout the country, visiting famous Taoist mountains and sacred places. His friends included the great T'ang dynasty poets Li Po and Wang Wei, and he would often be seen with them floating down the river singing and composing poetry.

The T'ang dowager empress was so impressed with Ssu-ma Ch'eng-chen's knowledge of the arts of longevity that she appointed him her spiritual adviser. Ch'eng-chen was not attracted to court life, and after a few months in the capital, he asked for permission to return to the life of a common citizen.

The T'ang emperor was also interested in the Taoist arts. Once, after Ch'eng-chen had left the palace, the emperor invited him back and asked him, "How can I cultivate the Tao?"

Ssu-ma Ch'eng-chen replied, "Minimize your desire, embrace simplicity, and practice noninterference."

The emperor said, "These principles are good for cultivating myself, but can they be used to govern a country?"

"Ruling the country begins with cultivating the self," answered Ch'eng-chen. "If your mind is clear and if you are free from desire, then the nation will naturally be prosperous and the people will be contented."

The emperor was very impressed with this answer. He sighed and said, "This is exactly what Kuang-ch'eng Tzu told the Yellow Emperor." He then asked Ssu-ma Ch'eng-chen to remain at the palace to be his adviser, but the sage declined, saying, "Court life is not for me."

As his fame as a Taoist sage grew, Ssu-ma Ch'eng-chen was approached by scholars, government officials, and Taoist practitioners, all of whom wanted to learn from him. Not liking the publicity, he went into the mountains and became a hermit. Eventually, he settled on Mount T'ien-tai.

One day, Ssu-ma Ch'eng-chen saw Lu Tsang walking up the mountain path to his hut. Lu Tsang was a Taoist adept and a friend of Ch'eng-chen's from their younger days. But whereas Ssu-ma Ch'eng-chen had decided to retreat from worldly affairs, Lu Tsang had accepted an appointment in the government.

On reaching the hut, Lu Tsang inquired, "Why didn't you build your retreat on Chung-nan Mountain? It's where all the Taoist hermits go."

Ch'eng-chen replied, "Chung-nan is too crowded with people who see the Taoist lifestyle as the short path to fame and political power."

When Lu Tsang heard this, he was ashamed. Chung-nan Mountain had acquired a reputation of being the "home" of sages, and many Taoist practitioners, including Lu Tsang, had chosen to settle there, hoping that they would attract the emperor's attention and receive an appointment.

About the same time that Ch'eng-chen retreated to Mount T'ien-tai, a Taoist practitioner from Manchuria by the name of Chiao Ching-chen was searching for the islands of immortality in the eastern oceans. He encountered a hermit on a small island who told him, "You need not journey across the sea to find the islands of immortality. Return to China and find the sage Ssu-ma Ch'eng-chen. He can show you the path to immortality."

After much searching, Chiao Ching-chen found Ssu-ma Ch'eng-chen and became his student. He completed his training and flew off to the immortal realm.

Surprised that he should attain immortality before his teacher, Ching-chen asked the celestial lords, "Why is my teacher Ch'eng-chen still in the mortal realm?"

The celestial lords responded, "Ssu-ma Ch'eng-chen is destined to reach the highest level of immortality. The reason that he is still in the mortal realm is because he needs to complete his books. If he left now, many generations of people would not attain the Tao."

When Ssu-ma Ch'eng-chen was about eighty years old, he and his friend Wen Ching were invited to a Taoist festival. The two men stayed in adjoining rooms in a guest house. In the middle of the night, Wen Ching was awakened by sounds of children chanting. He sat up, listened again, and discovered that the sounds were coming from

Ssu-ma Ch'eng-chen's room. He went outside and looked through his friend's window. To his shock, he saw a large bright disk hovering over Ch'eng-chen's head.

Wen Ching returned to his room and said to himself, "I've heard that the Mudball Cavity in the head of the highest adepts is capable of emitting celestial voices and sounds. I have known Ssu-ma Ch'eng-chen all this time, and I never knew he had attained such a high level of cultivation!"

When Ssu-ma Ch'eng-chen was eighty-nine years old, he called his students together and said, "I can see celestial messengers coming to invite me to the immortal lands. Continue to practice diligently; I hope to see you all in the immortal realm." He then sat in a meditation posture, closed his eyes, and liberated his spirit.

His students took his body and buried it on Mount T'ien-tai. When news of Ssu-ma Ch'eng-chen's departure from the mortal realm reached the palace, the emperor honored the great sage by writing an epitaph on his tomb.

SSU-MA CH'ENG-CHEN lived during the T'ang dynasty (618–906 CE) and is regarded as one of the greatest patriarchs of the Shang-ch'ing School of Taoism. He wrote many treatises on meditation and is responsible for introducing the technique of insight meditation (or internal gazing) into Taoist practice.

16
Minister from the Mountains
T'ao Hung-ching

T'ao Hung-ching was born into a poor but educated family. It is said that when he was conceived, a green dragon descended into his mother's womb and two immortals offered her incense.

Learning was important in the T'ao family, and all the children were instructed in the Confucian and Taoist classics. By the age of ten, Hung-ching was adept at music, astronomy, geography, military strategy, metallurgy, and

T'ao Hung-ching (left) and student.

the martial arts. However, his favorite book was Ko Hung's text on the arts of longevity and immortality titled *Pao-p'u Tzu* (*The Sage Who Embraces Simplicity*).

When his mother pressed him to enter the civil service, T'ao Hung-ching reluctantly accepted a post in the provincial government. However, after his mother passed away, he decided to leave the world of politics forever. He returned his official's robes to the local governor and asked the emperor for permission to retire. By then, Hung-ching was already well known as a Taoist adept and was admired by many. The emperor not only respected Hung-ching's wishes and permitted him to leave his post, but gave him a monthly stipend of cloth, grain, and vegetables. With these gifts and endowments, Hung-ching was able to retire from public life and study the Taoist arts.

Leaving the city, he built a retreat on Mount Mao. He adopted the lifestyle of a hermit, signed his letters with a pseudonym, and traveled deep into the mountains to look for ingredients to make the pill of immortality. When not working in his laboratory, he would play his flute or write poetry.

As T'ao Hung-ching's fame as a sage began to spread, many people came to his retreat asking to be accepted as students. Some were sincere in their pursuit of the Tao, but most were just curious to meet the Taoist hermit. Hung-ching found the visitors distracting, so he built a two-story house, made the lower level into a dormitory for his students, and retreated to the upper level where he would not be disturbed by nosy guests. Anyone who wanted to see Hung-ching had to relay their messages through a student. This arrangement drove the casual visitors away, and Hung-ching was able to work and study in peace.

One day, a student who had been buying supplies in the

city returned to tell his teacher, "The king of Ch'i has been overthrown. The new king has named his dynasty Liang. I wonder if he'll be as friendly to us as our old benefactor." Hung-ching said nothing.

The founder of the Ch'i dynasty (T'ao Hung-ching's original benefactor) had been succeeded by several weak and corrupt rulers. During the last years of the Ch'i dynasty, T'ao Hung-ching had written a poem that alluded to the rise of a new dynasty named Liang. When the founder of the Liang dynasty discovered this, he decided to honor the sage with gifts and endowments.

Several months after the news of the new dynasty had come, a messenger from the king of Liang arrived at the retreat. When T'ao Hung-ching came out to receive him, the messenger bowed and said, "My lord has asked me to thank you for giving him the confidence to become the son of heaven. He also said that if there is anything that he can help you with, you should not hesitate to ask."

The sage thanked him and said, "Please tell your lord that all I did was write a poem. I am a hermit who has spent many years trying to make the pill of immortality. I've got the equipment and the formulas; all I'm missing are some rare ingredients that can only be found in the mountains. If his majesty can assist me in completing my project, I will be most grateful."

The king of Liang immediately gave T'ao Hung-ching a large endowment of funds. He even provided a special writ that allowed the sage to travel unhindered anywhere in the kingdom to search for herbs and minerals.

One day, the king himself paid a visit to T'ao Hung-ching's retreat. Impressed with Hung-ching's wisdom and breadth of learning, the king begged the Taoist to become his chief minister. Hung-ching had anticipated this, so he took out a scroll, unrolled it, and presented it to the king. On the scroll was a painting of two oxen, one cropping grass leisurely on the hillside and the other imprisoned inside a golden cage. When the king saw the painting, he understood immediately and said, "You want to be free from the confines of the world. I will respect your wish and not ask for your service again."

Although he never took office, T'ao Hung-ching maintained a friendly relationship with several generations of the kings of Liang. This earned him the nickname "the Minister from the Mountains."

With the help of the royal endowment, T'ao Hung-ching finally succeeded in making the pill of immortality. At the time, he was seventy years old, but his complexion resembled that of a youth. He took the pill, expecting to ascend to immortality. Nothing happened. At first, he thought the pill was defective, but when one of his students ingested the pill and flew off to the immortal realm, he was bewildered. When the student returned after a sojourn in the celestial lands, Hung-ching said to him, "Next time when you visit the immortal realm, please ask the guardians why I could not attain immortality."

Several days later, the student visited the celestial lands again and returned with this message from the lords of heaven: "T'ao Hung-ching is not allowed to enter the immortal lands at this time because he has killed many insects and worms while searching for the ingredients for the pill. Therefore, he must wait another twelve years in the mortal realm before he can become an immortal."

T'ao Hung-ching took the message to heart. For the next twelve years, he abstained from meat and was careful not to step on insects and worms.

When he was eighty-five, he realized that his time in the

mortal realm was over. Hung-ching purified himself, lit a stick of incense, sat in a meditative posture, and shed his bodily shell. It is said that when the sage's spirit entered the immortal realm, the room was filled with fragrance and a golden light hovered in the chamber for three days.

T'AO HUNG-CHING lived during the period of the Six Dynasties (420–589 CE) and is regarded as one of the greatest patriarchs of the Shang-ch'ing School of Taoism. Adept at all aspects of the Taoist arts, he wrote over eighty treatises on topics that included alchemy, meditation, metallurgy, astronomy, geography, military strategy, divination, and medicine.

17
The First Disciple of Taoism

Wen Shih

It is said that when Wen Shih was born, a purple cloud descended into his mother's chamber and lotus flowers blossomed in the gardens. Even as a child, Wen Shih was interested in Taoist philosophy, astronomy, and celestial divination. He absorbed the essence of the Tao in the sun, moon, and stars; cultivated his virtue; and hid his wisdom.

Wen Shih served in the court of the Chou emperor as an astronomer. One night, as he was charting the course of the stars, he saw a purple vapor rising out of the east. Tracking it across the sky, he noticed that it was moving gradually toward the west. "A sage is journeying west and will soon reach the border town at Han Ku Pass," he said. "I want to be there to meet him."

The next morning, Wen Shih asked for permission to leave the court observatory and be assigned to the garrison at Han Ku Pass. When he arrived at his new post, he summoned his subordinate, Hsü Chia, and said to him, "If you see anyone extraordinary entering the town, let me know immediately."

Not long after Shih had settled in the frontier town, Lao Tzu arrived riding a blue ox. Hsü Chia hurriedly went to his superior and said, "A strange man riding a blue ox is coming to our town."

Wen Shih was delighted. He went to the city gates, bowed to Lao Tzu, and said, "Today I have the honor of meeting a sage. Please allow me to offer you the hospitality of my town."

Lao Tzu thanked Wen Shih and replied, "I'm just an old man who is leaving his old home in the east to live in his new home in the west."

But Shih persisted, "Honored One, when I saw a purple vapor in the sky moving from east to west, I knew that a great teacher would arrive in this town. Please stay and teach me about the Tao."

"What makes you think I'm the person you're looking for?" inquired Lao Tzu.

"It was last winter in the tenth month that I first saw the purple vapor in the sky," answered Shih. "After some calculations, I deduced that it would arrive here this month. Last night, I also saw dragons and serpents hovering over Han Ku pass. All these signs tell me that the great sage will arrive today."

Lao Tzu smiled and said, "I have heard about your ability to read omens and divine the future. You have the potential to understand the Tao and help others along the path."

Wen Shih bowed again. "May I have the honor of knowing your name?"

Lao Tzu replied, "I have many names, for I have appeared in many incarnations. I have taught the Yellow Emperor as well as the kings Yao, Shun, and Yü. In my current incarnation I am named Li Erh."

That night, Wen Shih honored Lao Tzu with a feast. After the banquet, he prostrated himself before the sage and formally asked to be accepted as a student. Lao Tzu stayed in the border town for a hundred days and taught Wen Shih the arts of the Tao.

When it was time for his teacher to leave, Wen Shih declared, "I would like to accompany you on your journey and serve you."

Lao Tzu refused, saying, "Although your roots are deep, you are not ready to climb with me to the clouds or fly to the four directions. You have a good understanding of the teachings, but you are still lacking in experience. When you can merge with the natural way, go to Szechwan and look for a blue ox. The ox will show you where to find me." He then dictated a book of five thousand words to his student. This book was the *Tao-te-ching*.

Wen Shih built a tower at Han Ku Pass and devoted himself to practicing what he had learned from Lao Tzu. One day, he looked at the sky and saw bands of multicolored clouds circling the North Star. When tendrils of starlight came through the window of Shih's meditation chamber and alighted on him, he knew that it was time for him to travel to Szechwan and find his teacher.

When Shih arrived in Szechwan, he began to ask people if they had seen a blue ox. "This man is insane," the citizens whispered to each other. "Who has ever seen an ox with a blue hide?"

Shih was not disappointed, however, and continued his search. One day, as he was resting by the road, he saw a young cowherd walking down the hillside leading a blue ox. Shih ran to the boy and said, "Can you please tell me who the owner of this ox is?"

The cowherd replied, "My lady has a child who loves this ox. The ox ran away two days ago. Since then my young master has not stopped crying."

When Wen Shih heard this, he was delighted. He said to the boy, "When you see your young master, please tell him that Wen Shih has arrived."

The cowherd took the ox to his master and said, "Wen Shih asked me to tell you that he has arrived." The child jumped up, clapped his hands, and said, "He's finally here! Invite him in at once."

When Wen Shih stepped into the mansion, the child was transformed into Lao Tzu. Thousands of rays of golden light emanated from his body, and a purple aura glowed around his head. A canopy emerged from the ground, and inside the pavilion was a seat surrounded by lotus flowers.

The old man walked to the chair, sat down, and said to Wen Shih, "When I left you, you were but a novice who aspired to cultivate the Tao. Today, I see a man with the air of an immortal. Your spirit has journeyed to the purple chamber of the Celestial Palace; you have merged with the North Star; and your name has been entered into the roster of the immortals."

When Lao Tzu finished speaking, the room was suddenly filled with celestial messengers and immortals. Wen Shih stepped onto a cloud and was escorted into the immortal realm by the personal attendants of the highest lords of heaven.

WEN SHIH, also known as Wen Tzu, lived in the latter part of the Chou dynasty (1122–221 BCE). He is reputed to be the first student of Lao Tzu and is the author of the Taoist classic *Wen Tzu*.

PART THREE

Magicians

張道陵

18
The Celestial
Teacher
Chang Tao-ling

Chang Tao-ling stood over seven feet tall and had bushy eyebrows, a large round forehead, and a hawk-beak nose. On the sole of his right foot were seven black dots arranged in the pattern of the seven stars of the Big Dipper. He had long, powerful arms that came down to his knees, and he walked with the strength of a tiger and the speed of a dragon.

Just before Chang Tao-ling was conceived, his mother dreamed that she saw a giant descending from the North Star. The lord of the North Star came toward her and gave her a flower. When she awoke the next morning, she smelled wisps of fragrance in her room and discovered that she had conceived a child. The fragrance lasted throughout the ten months she carried the baby in her womb.

On the day Chang Tao-ling was born, a yellow cloud covered the house and purple mist hovered about his mother's bedchamber. When he came out of his mother's womb, music and fragrance filled the air, and the room was flooded with light that matched the brilliance of the sun and moon.

Chang Tao-ling was exceptionally intelligent. At seven, he understood the teachings of Lao Tzu's *Tao-te-ching*. By twelve, he had mastered the *I-ching* and the classics of divination. As a young man, Tao-ling served his community as a provincial administrator, but he continued to study the arts of the Tao.

One day, while he was meditating in his retreat, a white tiger came to his side. In its mouth was a scroll of sacred scripture. Chang Tao-ling knew that it was time for him to leave the world of politics to pursue the Tao.

He resigned his position as civil administrator and became a hermit in the mountains. When the emperor heard about Chang Tao-ling's retirement, he offered him the title of "imperial teacher" and begged him to return to government service. Three times the emperor invited him, and each time Chang Tao-ling refused.

When Chang Tao-ling realized that he would not be left in peace, he moved to the remote and mountainous region of Szechwan. There, where the streams ran deep and the waterfalls cascaded down precipitous cliffs, he selected a cave where he could meditate, learn the arts of immortality, and attain the Tao.

Tao-ling stayed in his cave for many years until one day he heard the cry of a white crane. He knew it was a sign that he would attain enlightenment soon. A year later, when he was stoking the fires of his furnace to incubate the Dragon-Tiger Elixir, a red shaft of light appeared and illuminated the cavern. Another year went by, and a white tiger and a green dragon came into the cave and sat by the side of the cauldron to protect the elixir. Finally, three years after Chang Tao-ling had heard the call of the white crane, the elixir was completed and he became an immortal.

Tao-ling left his cave and traveled throughout the river valleys and mountains of Szechwan. On one of his journeys he met Lao Tzu, who taught him how to fly to the stars and tunnel under the earth. When Lao Tzu departed, he gave his pupil a scroll of talismans that had the power to heal the sick and a magic sword that could drive away malevolent spirits.

As time went on, Chang Tao-ling's skill in the arts of sorcery matured. Soon he could make himself invisible or change himself into any shape he wished. He could hear and see over great distances and could call down rain and snow. He could heal the sick and drive away evil spirits. His fame spread far and wide, and people called him the Celestial Teacher, for they believed that he was an immortal from the celestial realm.

When six evil spirits were wreaking havoc in Szechwan, Lao Tzu appeared to Chang Tao-ling and told him to return there to capture the spirits and bring them to judgment. Tao-ling secluded himself for one thousand days to prepare for this encounter.

When the six lords of evil heard that Chang Tao-ling was preparing to fight them, they gathered a large army of ghosts, ghouls, zombies, and other evil creatures. Meanwhile, the immortal also made preparations. He selected a green mound outside the city of Cheng-tu and built a tower with an altar in the middle. On the altar he placed objects of power, such as magical mirrors, bells, and talismans.

At the hour of *tzu* (11:00 PM), Chang Tao-ling ascended the tower and invoked the wind, rain, and thunder to beat upon the army of the evil spirits. He also drew talismans of power and called on the celestial deities to fight the evil forces. The lords of evil sent flaming spears and arrows to hit Chang Tao-ling, but none of them could harm him. As the deadly missiles flew toward him, he waved his sword of power, and they were transformed into lotus flowers.

The lords of evil then sent an army of hungry ghosts to attack Chang Tao-ling, but when they reached the altar, the immortal drew a talisman, and all the ghosts fell on their knees and begged for compassion. Next the six evil lords sent an army of ghouls, vampires, and zombies to attack Chang Tao-ling. When these creatures came near the altar, he rang his magical bells, and the undead clutched their ears and fell to the ground, never to rise again.

Seeing their minions had failed, the lords of evil came forward themselves to attack Chang Tao-ling, who grasped his sword and drew the Great Seal of Power. The sword emitted a stream of bright light that was transformed into a net. The net descended over the six evil spirits and formed a cage around them. When the evil ones saw their captor striding toward them with his sword of power, they begged for mercy and forgiveness. Tao-ling said to them, "You have brought illness and suffering to many people, and for these evil deeds, you must be punished. But, as the Celestial Way is compassionate, I will not kill you. I will, however, punish you by keeping you locked inside the depths of a mountain. In this way you will not harm people again."

When the people saw that the six lords of evil had been captured, they went to thank Chang Tao-ling and asked him to teach them his magic. He did not want to turn them away, so he told them to organize themselves into groups to help people who were in need. He also told them that the most effective way to fight evil was to do good deeds. If everyone did only what was good, evil could not take hold.

To his close followers, Chang Tao-ling taught the magic of talismans and told them to always use the power of sorcery for good, never for evil. On the day he ascended to the celestial realm, he left the sword of power and the Great Seal to his son and entrusted him to teach and lead the followers of the Celestial Teachers' Way.

CHANG TAO-LING lived during the latter part of the Han dynasty (206 BCE–219 CE). He founded the School of Taoism known as T'ien-shih Tao (the Celestial Teachers' Way) and is regarded as the father of organized religious Taoism.

19
The Wandering Healer
Fei Chang-fang

Fei Chang-fang had been interested in the Taoist arts ever since he was a child. He served as a police officer in the marketplace of a small town, but when he realized that he did not want to pursue a career in the government, he resigned.

One day not long after this, Chang-fang saw an old man arrive in the marketplace. The man went to a quiet corner, took some medicinal herbs out of a large gourd, and sat

Fei Chang-fang (left) and the old man in the gourd.

down on the ground to wait for customers. Fascinated by the old man's demeanor, Chang-fang watched him all day from the terrace of a restaurant. At the end of the day, after the other merchants had left, the old man gathered up his herbs and, to Chang-fang's surprise, jumped inside the gourd.

After watching the stranger's behavior for several days, Fei Chang-fang's curiosity got the better of him. He walked over to the old man's herb stand, but before he could speak a word of greeting, the old man dived into the gourd.

Chang-fang peered inside and saw a large hall decorated with silks and tapestries. A table was set in the middle of the chamber, and on the table was food and wine. Presently, the old man came toward Chang-fang and said, "Ordinary people cannot see me enter the gourd. Since you can, you must have the potential to learn magic." The old man then invited Chang-fang into his home for dinner. The younger man found that he too could fit inside the gourd.

Fei Chang-fang and the old man in the gourd soon became good friends. Daily, the younger man would visit the herb seller in the gourd and discuss the mysteries of the Tao.

One evening, the old man confided to Chang-fang, "I am an immortal who has broken the laws of heaven. I'm here because the celestial lords have ordered me to make amends by selling herbs and healing people in the mortal realm." Laughing, he continued, "My 'prison term' will be over tomorrow and I will be returning to the lands of immortality."

His young friend was sad when he heard this and said, "Since this is our last night together, let's get drunk and forget about the sadness of parting."

That evening, Fei Chang-fang invited the old man to his favorite restaurant and ordered a large keg of wine. When the old man saw that the waiters could not lift the barrel, he walked over, hefted the keg effortlessly over his shoulder, and set it on their table.

The two men drank all night long. When dawn broke, the old man said to Chang-fang, "I know that you want to learn the Taoist arts, so I'm going to invite you to come with me to the immortal lands to be my apprentice."

Chang-fang was tempted to accept the old man's offer. He thought for a moment and said, "I've always wanted to learn the Taoist arts and now I've been given the opportunity. I'd like to go with you, but I don't want my parents to worry about me while I'm gone."

The immortal said, "I have a solution for that."

Early the next morning, the old man accompanied Fei Chang-fang to his home. The immortal tied a rope to a bamboo stick and hung it on a tree. "Stay and watch," he told Chang-fang.

Not long after sunrise, the young man's parents came out of the house and saw their son hanging from the tree. They wept bitterly, took the body down, and prepared it for burial. All this time, Chang-fang was standing nearby watching. He tried to tell his parents that he wasn't really dead, but he found they could not hear him. He tried to put his hand on his father's shoulder, but his parents acted as if nothing had happened. Chang-fang slowly turned away and followed the old man into the mountains.

The immortal led him into a cave and said, "Sit down on this slab of rock."

When Chang-fang had settled himself on the rock, the old man hung a large boulder over his pupil's head. Then he conjured up snakes that began to bite at the rope with their sharp fangs. Soon the rope began to fray, and the boulder was suspended by only one thin strand. When

Chang-fang continued to sit on the rock as if nothing was happening, the old man said, "Not bad. You have the potential to learn magic and divination."

The next day, the old man conjured up a pile of feces that was covered with maggots. He picked up three maggots and told Chang-fang to eat them. At this, Chang-fang shuddered. The old man sighed and said, "Your foundation is not strong enough to learn the arts of immortality. You will become a powerful magician and diviner, but you are not destined to attain the highest level of immortality."

Fei Chang-fang replied, "I don't mind if I cannot become a high immortal. All I want is to be able to use what I have learned to help others."

"You have a good heart," said the old man. "I will give you two gifts." He handed Chang-fang a bamboo stick and said, "This stick can help you travel thousands of miles in a day. Tap it gently on the ground, say where you want to go, and it will take you there." Then he handed the young man a gourd and said, "This is my medicinal gourd. It is yours now. In it you will find medicines that can cure all kinds of illnesses." Then the old man disappeared, never to be seen again.

As Fei Chang-fang walked down the mountain, he said to himself, "I wonder how my parents are doing. I should go home and let them know that I'm still alive." He tapped the bamboo stick on the ground and spoke the name of his destination. Immediately, he was transported to his parents' home. He knocked on the door and found his father staring at him.

Chang-fang stared back and thought, "This is strange. My father has aged tremendously."

He was still staring when the older man exclaimed, "I

must be going insane. I'm seeing a ghost in broad day-light.''

Chang-fang comforted him and said, "I never died. I fol-lowed an immortal into the mountains to learn the Taoist arts.''

"But we buried you," said his father.

"You buried a bamboo stick," replied the son. "If you don't believe it, we can open up the grave and find out.''

So Chang-fang led his parents to his grave, dug up the coffin, and opened it. Inside was a bamboo stick.

The old couple arranged a banquet to celebrate their son's homecoming. When Chang-fang saw his relatives, he was amazed that they had all aged considerably. Astonished, he said, "I've only been away for several weeks. How is it that all of you have aged so much.''

His mother replied, "You left us for fifteen years.''

Fei Chang-fang suddenly realized that the weeks that he had spent in the immortal realm were equivalent to fifteen years in the realm of mortals.

After the banquet, he said to his parents, "I have to leave soon because I've pledged to use what I have learned to help others. I will try to come back and see you now and then." The next day, after making arrangements to have someone take care of his parents, he left.

Fei Chang-fang traveled throughout the countryside healing the sick and driving out evil spirits. He dispensed medicine from his gourd, exorcised ghosts, and helped towns and villages ward off floods and droughts.

He arrived in one village at midnight. Unable to find lodgings at the inn, he walked to the mansion of a well-to-do family and knocked on the door. A man with a kindly face opened the gate and said, "No one should be out at this time. Are you lost? Do you need a place to stay?''

"The inns are full," explained Chang-fang. "Will you let me stay at your house for the night? I'll gladly pay the expenses."

The owner of the mansion, whose name was Huan Ching, happened to be interested in the Taoist arts. Seeing that Fei Chang-fang was dressed in the robes of a wandering Taoist healer, he said, "You need not pay me anything. I will be honored to have you in my house."

The next morning, Huan Ching introduced Fei Chang-fang to his family and served up a sumptuous meal for his guest. While the two men discussed the Taoist arts over food and wine, Chang-fang noticed a dark vapor moving menacingly toward the Huan mansion.

Quickly, he said to his host, "There is a vapor of death coming toward your home. You must take your family and servants and go up to the mountains tomorrow before sunrise. Don't return home until sunset, or you will all die."

Huan Ching was puzzled. He said, "All my life I have tried to follow the Tao and help others. Have I done something wrong for such a disaster to come to my family?"

Fei Chang-fang replied, "It is because I know that you are a kind and virtuous man that I've given you the warning. There are some things that even the lords of heaven cannot control."

Huan Ching asked no more. He called his wife, children, and servants together, and said, "Pack some clothes and food. We need to leave for the mountains immediately."

When the household passed through the town on their way to the mountains, the neighbors laughed and said, "There goes a fool who listens to cheap advice from Taoist magicians." Huan Ching and his family ignored the jeers and left the village.

The next day after sunset, they returned to find a large

crowd standing outside their house. People were pointing to the stables behind the mansion and whispering to each other, "Did you hear that all the horses and oxen died yesterday? Even the sheep and the chickens in the barns are dead."

It was only then that Huan Ching realized that he and his family had escaped a major catastrophe. He thanked the lords of heaven and pledged to take offerings to the mountain shrines every year on the ninth day of the ninth month, for that was the day that his household had been spared from death. As the years went by, all the villages and towns in the area made it a custom to visit the mountain shrines on the ninth day of the ninth month.

Although Fei Chang-fang never entered the immortal realm, he lived a long life and never tired of healing and helping those in need. Following his example, many wandering healers began to carry their herbs and medicines in a gourd. And so it was that the gourd became the symbol of those who practiced the healing arts.

FEI CHANG-FANG lived during the latter part of the Han dynasty (206 BCE–219 CE) and is regarded as the patron of healers and herbalists. Huan Ching's visit to the shrines has become a cultural tradition of China. Today, it is still customary for many Chinese to spend a day in the mountains on the ninth day of the ninth lunar month.

20
The Sorcerer Strategist
Kiang Tzu-ya

Kiang Tzu-ya was born into a poor family. Abandoned and left to die, he was miraculously kept alive and cared for by dogs, cats, horses, and oxen. One day, a noblewoman, whose family name was Kiang, saw the infant being suckled by a cow and said, "This must be a special child." She took the infant home, adopted him, and named him Tzu-ya.

The boy grew up to be extraordinary. By the age of ten, he had mastered the arts of military strategy, divination, magic, astronomy, and geography. At eighteen, he left home to search for teachers to instruct him in the arts of longevity and immortality.

On one of his journeys, Tzu-ya met a celestial lord who told him, "You are not meant to live in the immortal lands. Your destiny is to help end the cruel rule of the Shang emperor. Use your gifts to advise the man who will become the new ruler."

Kiang Tzu-ya returned home. As he entered the courtyard, a servant ran to him and said, "Duke Chi is waiting for you in the guest reception hall."

"Tell the duke I won't be able to see him," replied Tzu-ya. "I'm going fishing today."

Far from being angered by Kiang Tzu-ya's behavior, the duke simply responded to his refusal by saying, "If it is inconvenient for Master Kiang, I will come another day."

Three times Duke Chi asked to see Kiang Tzu-ya and each time Tzu-ya refused to meet him. On the duke's fourth visit, Tzu-ya came out. He bowed before his guest, asked for forgiveness, and said, "The fortunes of the nation are a matter of life and death. Before I can offer you my service, I need to know if you are indeed the man destined to be the next emperor."

Duke Chi was shocked. He had come to ask Kiang Tzu-ya for advice on running the day-to-day affairs of his fief and had not expected to discuss "treasonous" matters. The duke's reaction confirmed Kiang Tzu-ya's faith in him. Duke Chi was a benevolent, kind, and humble man who had no ambitions of becoming emperor. Tzu-ya did not want to see one power-hungry ruler replaced by another.

He tried to persuade Duke Chi that it was time to end the rule of the cruel emperor Shang Ts'ou, but the duke was hesitant.

"Many people will die if we fight Ts'ou," he protested.

"More are dying under his rule," replied Tzu-ya.

Eventually, it was Shang Ts'ou's own actions that convinced Duke Chi that the emperor must be removed. Jealous of Chi's popularity with the nobility and the citizens, Shang Ts'ou had Duke Chi's son arrested and killed. Then, he summoned the duke and forced him to eat his son's flesh.

When Duke Chi returned to his fief, he approached Kiang Tzu-ya and said, "It is time to get rid of this evil ruler."

Duke Chi's campaign against the emperor is dramatized in the novel *Feng-shen yen-yi (Investiture of the Deities)*. The following excerpt from the novel describes how Kiang Tzu-ya used his magic to defeat the evil emperor of Shang.

Tzu-ya instructed his assistant to build a mound about three feet high. When it was completed, Tzu-ya climbed to the top of the mound and undid the knot in his hair. With a sword in his hand, he faced east toward the direction of the K'un-lun Mountains and prostrated. Then he walked the steps of the Big Dipper and began his magic ritual.

Soon a strong wind blew and whistled through the forest. Dust churned up from the ground and nothing could be seen. The sky darkened and the earth rumbled. In the distance, the waves crashed onto the shore and the mountains shook. Bells and chimes on the prayer flags clanged against each other. All who stood nearby were unable to open their eyes.

Far away, in the enemy camp, the weather was warm and there were only small gusts of wind. The commanding generals said among themselves, "This is a good sign. Even the weather is on our side. Our emperor has the favor of the celestial lords, for they have sent this refreshing wind to cool us on the march."

However, as the armies of the evil emperor approached Tzu-ya's camp, the situation changed. Tzu-ya summoned a cold wind, and for three days it blew continuously. The imperial soldiers began to whisper to each other, "We are living in unfortunate times. It is said that the weather will become unpredictable when there are problems in the country."

An hour after that, a few snowflakes fluttered around. The imperial soldiers began to complain, "We are dressed in summer uniforms. How can we survive this cold?"

Not long after that, the snow became heavy, and the soldiers could hardly see what was in front of them. Now and then, they could hear avalanches crashing down the mountain slopes. The land became a wall of pure white. Wolves howled, their cries coming out of nowhere. The snow soon became ankle-deep, then knee-deep. The progress of the imperial army came to a halt.

The commanding general looked at his lieutenants and said, "I have never seen snow this heavy in the middle of summer." The general, an old man, was having a hard time enduring the cold. All the soldiers were huddled in heaps, stricken with cold. There was nothing their commanders could do to keep them moving.

Meanwhile, in Tzu-ya's camp, everyone was prepared for the snow. The soldiers stood in their ranks, grateful they were wearing padded jackets and straw hats. Everyone was awed by Tzu-ya's power.

Tzu-ya then asked his assistant, "How deep is the snow?"

The young man replied, "In the higher places, it is about two feet, but in the valley the drifts must be at least four or five feet."

Tzu-ya returned to the mound, undid the topknot in his hair, drew talismans in the air with his sword, and chanted. At once, the snow clouds disappeared and a bright sun shone. The ice and snow melted and a torrent of water rushed down the mountainsides into the valley. Just when the water had formed a lake in the valley, Tzu-ya changed his incantations. He drew another talisman and whipped up a cold wind. The sun disappeared behind ominous black clouds and the water froze immediately.

When Tzu-ya looked in the direction where the imperial army was stranded, he saw broken flags and banners. Turning to his assistant he said, "Lead twenty strong men into the enemy camp and capture the commanders.

After Shang Ts'ou was defeated, Duke Chi founded a new dynasty. He named it Chou and was crowned Emperor Wen. Kiang Tzu-ya was given the title of duke and received rich gifts of land and gold from the new ruler.

Emperor Wen appointed Tzu-ya his chief minister. Tzu-ya helped him rebuild the country, and when the nation had recovered from the harsh rule of the last Shang emperor, the magician retired.

Kiang Tzu-ya lived out the rest of his life in the fief that Emperor Wen had given him. He mingled with the common citizens in the marketplace and visited the hermits in the mountains. When visiting dignitaries asked for an audience, they were usually met by servants and told, "The master went out early in the morning with his fishing rod and a flask of wine and is not expected to return until sunset."

KIANG TZU-YA lived from the end of the Shang dynasty (1766–1122 BCE) to the beginning of the Chou dynasty (1122–221 BCE). He was Duke Chi's principal adviser during the latter's campaign against Shang Ts'ou and became the chief minister of the Chou dynasty when Chi was made emperor. Tzu-ya's treatise on strategy and tactics, *Kiang T'ai-kung ping-fa (Master Kiang's Art of War),* is considered one of the greatest classics of military strategy.

21
The Immortal in Sheep's Clothing
Tso Chi

Tso Chi learned the magical arts on a mountain called the Celestial Pillar. He was especially adept at shape-shifting and could summon ghosts and spirits.

The chief minister of the Han empire, Ts'ao Ts'ao, heard about Tso Chi's skills and wanted to meet him.

When Tso Chi arrived at court, the chief minister said, "Demonstrate to me some of your magical skills."

"It would be my pleasure," replied the magician.

After seeing some of the marvels Tso Chi could perform,

Ts'ao Ts'ao asked the magician if he could survive a year without food and water.

"Lock me in a cell and find out," replied Tso Chi.

After a year, when Tso Chi was released, the magician still looked well-fed and healthy.

One time, Ts'ao Ts'ao threw a large banquet that was attended by many high-ranking officials and diplomats. When food was brought to the tables, the chief minister remarked, "I would love to have carp from the Pine River tonight." Tso Chi took a bowl, threw a fishing line into it, and pulled out a carp. Everyone at the banquet was impressed.

Then Ts'ao Ts'ao said, "The carp won't taste good if we do not steam it with ginger from Szechwan."

"No problem," said Tso Chi, who immediately pulled some fresh Szechwan ginger from his sleeves.

Another time, Ts'ao Ts'ao and his friends were touring the countryside. At midday, they were all hungry. Ts'ao Ts'ao was about to order the servants to go to the nearest town to buy food when Tso Chi took out a piece of meat and a flask of wine from a basket. He distributed the meat and wine to all those present, and everyone ate to their heart's content.

After this incident, Ts'ao Ts'ao began to feel threatened by the Taoist magician. "He has so much power," thought the minister. "What if he decides to support my enemies?" So he secretly plotted to kill Tso Chi. But when Ts'ao Ts'ao's soldiers went to Tso Chi's home, the magician immediately vanished into a wall.

The following week, Ts'ao Ts'ao's spies reported seeing Tso Chi in the marketplace, but when the soldiers arrived, all the citizens there looked like Tso Chi. Not wanting to arrest the wrong person and anger the people, Ts'ao Ts'ao ordered the soldiers back to their barracks.

A few days later, the minister's spies again reported seeing Tso Chi, this time on a hillside near the city of Yang. Ts'ao Ts'ao immediately led his soldiers to kill the magician. When they arrived on the mountain, they saw Tso Chi disappear into a flock of sheep. Ts'ao Ts'ao now knew there was nothing he could do, so he told his men, "Forget about killing this man."

Hearing that, one of the sheep stood up on its hind legs and asked, "Is this true?"

Ts'ao Ts'ao immediately shouted, "Shoot him!" But before the soldiers could pull their bows, all the sheep were standing on their hind legs demanding, "Is this true?"

After that, Ts'ao Ts'ao gave up trying to kill Tso Chi. For his part, Tso Chi had had his fill of entertaining government officials. He left the capital and disappeared into the mountains.

Tso Chi lived during the latter part of the Han dynasty (206 BCE–219 CE) when Ts'ao Ts'ao was the chief minister and the power behind the throne. Ts'ao Ts'ao's son, Ts'ao Pei, eventually deposed the Han emperor and founded the Wei dynasty (220–265 CE).

22
The Spirit Catcher
Ko Hsüan

Ko Hsüan learned his magic from Tso Chi. Hsüan could make stone statues walk; he could talk to butterflies and grasshoppers and get them to dance; and he could grow vegetables in winter and create ice in summer.

Once, when Ko Hsüan and his friends wanted to draw water from a well to quench their thirst, they could not find a container. Hsüan pointed at the well and cups of water flew into their hands.

One year there was a drought. When the emperor asked Ko Hsüan if he could make rain, the magician took his writing brush, drew a talisman, and fastened it on top of his house. Soon, dark clouds appeared and rain began to fall.

Ko Hsüan was also adept at capturing evil spirits. One time, he heard that a group of mischievous spirits had taken over a shrine in a nearby village. The spirits made the villagers send food and offerings every day, threatening that accidents and mishaps would occur if the gifts did not arrive.

Hsüan went to the village, strode into the shrine, and saw the spirits perching on the beams and rafters.

"Put your offerings on the altar," demanded the spirits.

When Ko Hsüan did not respond, they whipped up gusts of wind and tried to blow him out of the shrine. When Hsüan continued to defy them, they pelted him with stones.

Eventually, Ko Hsüan said in a loud and authoritative voice, "Stop your mischief or I'll trap you in a gourd."

The spirits fluttered around the shrine and showed no signs of submission. Hsüan then drew a talisman in the air and said, "Capture!" The spirits were immediately sucked into the gourd.

Ko Hsüan stepped out of the shrine and was greeted by a crowd of villagers. He assured them, "I have captured the spirits. They won't bother you again." He then fastened a talisman on the door of the shrine and said, "This talisman will keep evil spirits away. Your village will be free from such mischief from now on."

Another time, Ko Hsüan was walking on the north slopes of Mount Hua when he noticed a dark vapor hovering over a house. Sensing that there was an evil spirit inside, he transformed himself into a farmer and knocked on the door.

A scholar welcomed him in, and Ko Hsüan said, "I need someone to help me with the harvest today."

"I will be glad to help you," replied the scholar.

Ko Hsüan led the scholar away from the house and said, "There is an evil snake spirit in your house posing as your wife. She has already eaten a lot of children in the village." When the scholar refused to believe him, Ko Hsüan took the man into the woods and showed him a pit filled with skulls and bones.

The scholar shook with fear and said, "What should I do?" Ko Hsüan said, "Tonight, you must occupy her attention so that I can capture her."

The scholar went into the village and bought a bolt of cloth. That evening, he presented it to his wife and tried to get her to talk about the clothes that she would make. Meanwhile, Ko Hsüan set up an altar outside the house, drew his talismans, and chanted incantations. When the woman realized that she had been trapped, she transformed herself into a large python and tried to swallow the scholar. Seeing this, Ko Hsüan drew his sword, threw it at the snake, and impaled it against the wall. Stench filled the room, and scorpions and centipedes crawled out of cracks in the wall to dissolve into a puddle of dark liquid.

Ko Hsüan drew another talisman, burned it, and told the scholar to eat the ashes. After the scholar swallowed the burned talisman, he began to vomit a thick yellow liquid. Hsüan said to him, "You were poisoned by the snake spirit. If you didn't have a spark of goodness in you, you would have become a vampire yourself."

When Hsüan knew that it was time for him to leave the mortal realm, he built a hut in the mountains and set up a furnace and a cauldron to make the elixir of immortality.

One winter day, he was out in the woods gathering roots and minerals, barefoot and dressed in a sleeveless shirt. Two daughters of a woodcutter, who were helping their father carry firewood home, saw him digging in the snowy ground. Not knowing that Ko Hsüan was a Taoist adept, the sisters said to each other, "This man doesn't even have shoes and a warm coat. We should help him."

One woman made a pair of shoes and the other made a wool shirt. They brought their gifts to Ko Hsüan's home and called to him, "Old man, we have brought you shoes and a coat."

When there was no answer, the sisters opened the door of the hut and walked in. Inside, they found a furnace with smoldering ashes, a cauldron, and a note that said, "I thank you for your gifts. If you open the cauldron, you will find two halves of a pill. These are my gifts to both of you."

The sisters found the pill and swallowed it. From that day on, the women stopped aging. They maintained their youth and vigor all their lives and lived for over a hundred years.

They also found a letter on a table. On the envelope was written, "An Invitation to the Immortal Ko from the Celestial Lords." It was then that they realized Ko Hsüan had ascended to immortality.

Ko Hsüan lived during the period of the Three Kingdoms (220–265 CE). He collected and edited the Ling-pao (Sacred Spirit) Scriptures, which are the earliest texts of the Taoist canon.

23
The People's Protector
Mah Ku

Mah Ku was the daughter of Mah Chiu, the mayor of a small town. One year, Mah Chiu was put in charge of building the city wall. Hoping to get a bonus for completing the project ahead of schedule, he made the townspeople work day and night.

Chiu called the citizens together and told them, "The city wall must be completed before winter. You are only allowed to rest during the time before the first rooster crow and sunrise."

The people murmured among themselves and said,

"This is autumn. How can we finish the wall before winter?" So they elected a spokesperson to appeal to the mayor. "We had a drought this summer. If we don't harvest the crops that are left, we'll starve in winter," said the representative.

Mah Chiu replied, "I have no time for this nonsense," and ordered the man to be flogged. When the governor of the region sent the people supplies of grain and salt, Mah Chiu sold them on the black market and pocketed the money.

Day after day, the people labored. Men, women, and even children were forced out of their homes to work on the city wall.

When Mah Ku tried to persuade her father to give the people more time to rest, she was told, "Don't bother in my affairs or I'll lock you in your room."

Mah Ku was an extraordinary woman. From the time she was a child, she could imitate the calls of every animal and bird. She could jump up walls, walk on rafters, and climb trees. She was so silent and stealthy that she often gave the impression of being in several places at once.

Seeing the people of her town dying from hunger and exhaustion, Mah Ku decided to help them. One night, she crept out of her father's mansion and climbed to the top of the house. There she imitated a rooster's crow. Then, quietly and quickly, she climbed onto another roof and crowed again. Soon all the roosters in the town were crowing. Although it was only midnight, the guards, hearing the sounds, allowed the people to return home. This went on for weeks until one morning Mah Chiu discovered that work on the city wall was way behind schedule.

He questioned the guards who said, "We followed your orders strictly and only let the people go when the roosters crowed." That night Mah Chiu stayed up to see what was going on. At midnight, he heard a rooster's cry from the roof of his house. Then he heard another one from a neighboring rooftop.

When Mah Ku returned to her room in the early hours of the morning, her father was there waiting for her.

Mah Chiu seized his daughter by the arm and said, "You have destroyed my chance of getting rich. Now, you're going to pay for it." Chiu tied his daughter to the bedpost and went to get a whip, but when he returned to the room, Mah Ku had disappeared.

Chiu and his guards searched the town and the surrounding countryside but could not find Mah Ku.

Not long after Mah Ku's escape, one of Mah Chiu's guards informed the governor that Chiu was stealing government supplies and selling them on the black market. Mah Chiu was arrested and sent to work in the imperial mines for the rest of his life.

While fleeing from her father, Mah Ku met an immortal who taught her the arts of magic and immortality. After she completed her apprenticeship, she returned to her village. There, on a stone bridge in front of a crowd of people, she flew up to the sky. The people of her town named that bridge Immortal's Bridge, in honor of the young woman's courage and integrity.

There is no information as to when Mah Ku lived.

24
Lady of the Great Mysteries
T'ai-hsüan Nü

T'ai-hsüan Nü was married to a man who did not love her. Soon after she gave birth to a son, her husband died.

One day, T'ai-hsüan Nü met a diviner in the marketplace who told her, "You and your son will not live long." When she heard this, she did not panic. Calmly and methodically, she began to study and practice the arts of immortality. After a few years, she stopped aging. When her son had a family of his own, she retreated to the mountains, built a hut, and began to gather minerals to make the elixir of immortality.

As her cultivation progressed, T'ai-hsüan Nü was able to sleep on the ice in winter and not be chilled, enter the water and not get wet, sit in a fire and not be burned, and be at different places at the same time.

Once, T'ai-hsüan Nü met two young men who were pulling a wagon on a mountain road. Inside the wagon was an old man covered with blankets. She overheard one of the young men say, "The snow has blocked the passes. If we don't get our father to the doctor by sunset, he'll die." She pointed at the snowdrifts, and the snow melted immediately, leaving the path clear.

Another time, she saw a man and a woman running from a group of bandits. She pointed toward the side of a mountain, and immediately a rock slide blocked the trail behind the couple, allowing them to escape.

Yet another time, when she saw a wildfire threatening a village, she blew at the flames and the fire disappeared. At a wave of her hand, the burned trees and grasses returned to life.

T'ai-hsüan Nü's reputation as a master of magic and the arts of immortality increased as more and more people witnessed her abilities. Many young women began to approach her, asking to be her students. Soon, she had gathered together a group of apprentices.

One day, T'ai-hsüan Nü and her students were collecting minerals and herbs in the mountains. At dusk, the apprentices began to whisper among themselves, "The sun is about to set. How can we make it home in the dark?"

Hearing their remarks, T'ai-hsüan Nü struck a rock wall with her walking stick. Immediately, the wall opened to reveal a large, dry cave. Inside the cave were beds, tables, and chairs. In one corner was a bundle of firewood, and in another a pot of soup and herbs was cooking over a stove.

T'ai-hsüan Nü lived to be over two hundred years old. Her complexion was always that of a young woman and her hair was smooth and black. One day, her students heard children's voices coming from their teacher's room. When they pushed open the door, they saw T'ai-hsüan Nü flying up to the sky accompanied by a group of immortals.

There is no information as to when and where T'ai-hsüan Nü lived.

25
The Woman Who Flew on a Toad

T'ang Kuang-chen

T'ang Kuang-chen was ill all the time when she was a child.
After she married, the illnesses got worse: she bled con-
stantly and was plagued with a variety of infections.

One night, Kuang-chen dreamed that a Taoist gave her
some medicine, which she took. When she awoke the next
morning, she found that her health problems had disappeared. At that moment, she decided she wanted to study
and practice the Taoist arts for the rest of her life.

She packed up a small bundle of belongings, said farewell
to her husband and mother, and went into the mountains.

While wandering in the forest, Kuang-chen met the female immortal Ho Hsien-ku, who taught her magic and the arts of immortality.

When T'ang Kuang-chen had completed her apprenticeship with Immortal Ho, she decided to return home to see her mother. On the way back to her village, she stopped at a town and found lodgings with a family by the name of Kuo.

While Kuang-chen was having dinner with her hosts, she heard someone call her name. She excused herself, went outside, and found three old men standing on a cloud. Immediately she summoned a giant toad, stepped onto its back, and flew to meet the three immortals. Delighted, the three old men took her on a tour of the famous mountains and lakes.

Flying over the K'un-lun Mountains, one of the immortals said to T'ang Kuang-chen, "Would you like to transcend the mundane and enter the sacred, shed your shell and become an immortal? Or would you rather keep your body and remain in the mortal realm?"

Kuang-chen replied, "It is my duty to look after my mother while she is still alive."

The immortals then said, "We understand that at this time you would like to keep your body and remain in the mortal realm." They gave her a pill and left.

Kuang-chen swallowed the pill. From that time on, she was immune to heat, cold, hunger, and thirst. She returned to her village to care for her aging mother and lived what appeared to be a normal life. After her mother passed away, T'ang Kuang-chen received an invitation from the celestial lords. She summoned the giant toad, got onto its back, and rode off to the immortal realm.

T'ANG KUANG-CHEN lived during the Sung dynasty (960–1279 CE). It is said that she learned the arts of female internal alchemy from Immortal Ho Hsien-ku, the patron of female Taoist cultivation. Kuang-chen wrote poems to document her spiritual experiences, and these writings are considered some of the finest expositions on female Taoist learning.

26
Immortal from the Sky
Tung-fang Shuo

When Tung-fang Shuo was a boy, he once left home and did not return until a year later. His family was worried, and when he came home eventually, his brother asked, "Where have you been? You were away for almost a year."

Tung-fang Shuo replied, "I was playing on the beach and got sprayed by the salt water. So I went to the Deep Spring to wash the salt off my clothes. I left home early in the morning and it's only lunchtime now. Why do you say I've been away for a year?"

His brother exclaimed, "The Deep Spring is ten thousand miles from here! It would take a normal person more than year to get there and back. You must be joking!"

When Tung-fang Shuo was twenty-two years old, he wrote a letter to Wu-ti, the Han emperor. In the letter, he explained, "I was orphaned at an early age and was brought up by my brother. I mastered the classics when I was twelve. At fifteen, I became an expert in the martial arts. At sixteen, I became a master poet and memorized twenty thousand lines of song. At nineteen, I mastered the science of warfare and the art of diplomacy. Now, at twenty-two, I stand head and shoulders above everyone. My body is strong and graceful. My mind is agile and cunning. I am honest and trustworthy, brave and honorable. I am someone whom your majesty should have in your service!"

Many people would have been offended by Tung-fang Shuo's manner of presenting himself, but the emperor realized that this was no ordinary person. He not only employed the young man in his service, but made Tung-fang Shuo his personal adviser.

The emperor valued Shuo's friendship and lavished him with gifts. He even sent a beautiful woman to be the young man's wife. However, every time the emperor sent gifts of silks and gold to his friend, Tung-fang Shuo turned all the gifts over to his wife. People made fun of his strange behavior and joked, "Either he really loves his wife or he is afraid of her!" But Shuo was not offended. He only laughed and said, "I am a hermit who escapes worldly matters by hiding in the palace!"

Often he would get drunk and sing in a loud voice:

> The world is too muddy,
> Therefore I hide behind the gates of the palace.

The palace is a place where I can cultivate my life,
Why I do I need to be a hermit in the deep
    mountains?

Before Tung-fang Shuo was to leave the mortal realm, he remarked to the emperor, "No one knows where I came from and where I will go. Only the astronomer who keeps a record of the stars knows my true identity."

A few days later, when Tung-fang Shuo was nowhere to be seen, the emperor was worried about his friend. Suddenly, remembering what the magician had said, he summoned the court astronomer and asked about Tung-fang Shuo.

The court astronomer was bewildered. He said, "Your majesty, I honestly do not know the man's true identity."

The emperor was a very clever man. He sensed that Tung-fang Shuo's identity must be related to the patterns of stars in the sky. Otherwise, he would not have mentioned that only the keeper of the record of the stars would know it.

Turning to the astronomer, the emperor asked, "In your observation of the stars during the last forty years, did you notice anything out of the ordinary?"

The astronomer replied, "My lord, I did notice that forty years ago, a star mysteriously disappeared and then a few days ago reappeared again."

The emperor finally understood. He sighed and said, "In the eighteen years that Tung-fang Shuo was with me, I did not even know that he was a sky immortal. What a pity!"

TUNG-FANG SHUO lived during the early part of the Han dynasty (206 BCE–219 CE) and served in the court of the emperor Wu Ti.

PART FOUR

Diviners

27

The Reader of Human Destiny

Chang Chung

Chang Chung learned the arts of divination from an immortal, and was especially adept at predicting events and reading personal destiny.

When Chu Yüan-chang, the leader of the rebellion against the Mongol rule, learned about Chang Chung's skills, he invited Chung to his military camp and requested, "Tell me about my future."

Chang Chung replied, "Everyone wants to drive out the Mongols and become emperor, but only one person will succeed. I believe that you are that person."

Chu Yüan-chang said, "What makes you say that?"

The other man replied, "You have the forehead of a dragon and the eyes of a phoenix. The destiny of kingship is written upon your face."

Delighted, the rebel leader begged, "Please stay and be my adviser. I need people like you if I am to defeat the Mongols."

Chang Chung agreed.

Not long after that, Chu Yüan-chang was fighting a rival rebel leader named Chen Yu-liang. Yu-liang was a formidable opponent who commanded a large and disciplined army. After a fierce battle in which both sides suffered severe losses, Chu Yüan-chang wanted to retreat. He sought out Chang Chung and said, "We've lost a large part of our army today. The soldiers are weak and morale is low. I think we should retreat and regroup before we fight again."

Chung replied calmly, "Chen Yu-liang was killed by an arrow not long ago. If we can get this news to his commanders, the victory will be ours."

"What should we do?" Chu Yüan-chang asked.

His adviser answered, "Prepare a eulogy and have a condemned prisoner read it at the front lines. When Yu-liang's troops hear it, they will lose their will to fight."

As Chang Chung had predicted, Chen Yu-liang's soldiers were demoralized once they learned their leader was dead. Without further resistance, Yu-liang's lieutenants either surrendered or fled.

Some months later, a general of Chu Yüan-chang's army named Hsü Ta asked Chang Chung about his destiny. Hsü Ta was a brilliant commander and a gifted strategist, and was extremely loyal to Yüan-chang.

Chung studied the general's face and said, "Your eyes are large and bright and you always look beyond the horizon. You will not only be rich and famous, but you will become the supreme commander of the imperial army." Hsü Ta was very happy, but before he could thank Chang Chung, the diviner added, "I'm afraid that you will not live beyond forty."

Hsü Ta said, "I will be content if I am given forty years. I only ask the lords of heaven that I live long enough to bring peace to the country." Chang Chung sighed and said to himself, "This man may die a violent death, but his honor and integrity will never be forgotten."

Chu Yüan-chang eventually defeated the Mongols and became the emperor of the Ming dynasty. Those who had helped him win the throne were rewarded with lands and titles. As Chang Chung had predicted, Hsü Ta became the supreme commander of the imperial army and was given the title the Martial Duke.

The new emperor asked Chang Chung to stay at his side and be his adviser. Chung declined but agreed to remain in the capital.

The years passed, and the country began to recover from the Mongols' harsh rule and civil unrest. One morning after a night of heavy rain, a guard hurried to the palace with news for the emperor. "Chang Chung has jumped off a bridge into the river and was swept away," he announced.

The emperor immediately ordered swimmers and divers into the river to search for Chang Chung. When his men failed to find the diviner or his body, Chu Yüan-chang told the imperial messengers, "Put a poster in every town announcing that I will give a large reward to anyone who has news of Chang Chung's whereabouts."

Six months later, a commander from one of the border garrisons asked for an audience with the emperor. The man bowed to Chu Yüan-chang and said, "Last spring I saw a man leaving our border. His features are identical to the man named Chang Chung."

"On exactly what date did you see this man?" the emperor questioned.

"The fifteenth day of the fourth month," the commander replied.

The emperor nodded thoughtfully. Chang Chung had jumped into the river on that day.

Toward the end of his reign, Chu Yüan-chang was afraid that his advisers and military commanders would overthrow him. So one by one, he had them eliminated. Hsü Ta, who was popular with both the nobility and the people, was one of the first victims. Knowing that Hsü Ta was deathly allergic to goose meat, Yüan-chang sent a gift of it to his general.

When Hsü Ta saw the meat, he sighed and said, "All my life I have been loyal. It is my duty to obey the emperor even if he wants me dead." As Chang Chung had predicted, Hsü Ta died before he was forty years old.

After Hsü Ta's death, most of Chu Yüan-chang's original supporters were either murdered or executed for treason. Chang Chung had managed to escape with his life only because he had noticed that during the last years of Yüan-chang's reign, the emperor's eyes had become aggressive, and a dark cloud of death had always hung over his forehead.

Chang Chung never returned to China. He left the lands controlled by Yüan-chang, wandered west, and lived out the rest of his days far from the empire he had once helped to create.

CHANG CHUNG lived from the end of the Yüan dynasty (1271–1368 CE) to the early Ming (1368–1644 CE). He helped Chu Yüan-chang defeat the Mongols and establish the Ming dynasty.

28

The Crane Immortal

Ch'ing Wu

Ch'ing Wu learned the Taoist arts from P'eng Tsu (P'eng the Ancient One), who was rumored to have discovered an elixir of immortality and to have lived for over a thousand years.

After he completed his apprenticeship, Ch'ing Wu built a hut on a rocky ledge on Mount Hua and lived in the company of the cranes and eagles that soared among the craggy peaks. The northern part of the mountains, where Ch'ing Wu had made his home, resembled a great dragon—the north peak was the head, the ridges were the spine, and the craggy spurs were the legs and talons. Clouds and mist swirled around the peaks and rocky escarpments, making the land seem elusive, mysterious, and ephemeral.

Living on Mount Hua, Ch'ing Wu saw that clouds and mists gathered only in certain places. He also noticed that some parts of the mountain were frequented by animals and birds more than others. One day, following the flight path of a crane, he climbed through a cleft in the rock and found a secluded valley. At the mouth of the valley was a round boulder, and in a pool sheltered by the boulder was a group of cranes.

As Ch'ing Wu approached them, the birds changed into human form. The crane that Ch'ing Wu had followed came toward him and said, "We are crane immortals, and we have waited for you for a long time. The lords of heaven have chosen you to be the keeper of the knowledge of the land and its power. Therefore, we will teach you how to recognize the flow of energy in the land and how to select grave sites that will make kings and sages out of the descendants of those who are buried there."

Ch'ing Wu bowed and replied, "I am honored to accept this responsibility, and I will promise that this knowledge will only be used for the purposes of good." He stayed with the crane immortals until he had learned everything they could teach him.

At that time, in a village in southeast China, lived a man named Sun Chung who grew and sold melons for a living. One hot summer day, while harvesting his melons, Chung saw three men walking down the road near his house. Being a kind and generous man, Sun Chung called to the strangers, saying, "It's too hot to travel when the sun is high. Come and have some watermelons. It will cool you down."

The three men thanked the farmer for his kindness and spent the afternoon resting in Chung's house. As the sun began to dip below the mountaintops, the men said, "We should be on our way, but before we leave, we would like to give you a gift. Follow us into the mountains and we'll show you a burial site."

Sun Chung followed them up the mountain path. The sun had set and a soft mist was beginning to gather in the valleys. The three mysterious strangers led Chung to a hidden spring on the side of the mountain and said, "When your mother dies, you should bury her here." Sun Chung gathered some rocks and built a cairn to mark the spot. When he tried to thank the three men, they changed into white cranes and flew away.

Sun Chung returned home. The years went by, but he did not forget his encounter with the crane immortals. One day, his mother called him to her room and said, "I do not have long to live. I will feel better leaving you if I know that you will continue the family line." Being a faithful son, Sun Chung understood her wish. Several months later, he introduced a plain-looking young woman, the daughter of a farmer, to his mother. A marriage agreement was made between the two families, and on a warm spring day before the rainy season, Sun Chung brought his bride home.

A year later, Chung's mother died. Remembering what the crane immortals had told him, he buried her in the spot marked by the rock cairn. Not long afterward, his wife conceived a child. When his son was born, Sun Chung named him Chien.

Sun Chien became a general of the Han empire, and when the ruling house became weak and corrupt, he took over the southeastern region of China and proclaimed himself king of the state of Wu. His descendants Sun T'se and Sun Ch'uan expanded the territories of Wu and fought the rulers of the kingdoms of Wei and Shu for the title of emperor of China.

The site where Sun Chung had buried his mother was a "kingmaker" site, and the crane immortals who had visited Chung were emanations from Ch'ing Wu.

CH'ING WU lived during the early Han dynasty (206 BCE–219 CE) and is considered by many to be the father of the art of k'an-yu (or feng-shui).

Sun Chung lived during the late Han dynasty. His son Sun Chien is regarded as the founder of the Wu dynasty in the era of the Three Kingdoms (220–265 CE). The Three Kingdoms were Wei, founded by Ts'ao Ts'ao's son Ts'ao Pei; Shu, founded by Lui Pei; and Wu, founded by Sun Chien.

29

The Mad Beggar

Chou Tien

Chou Tien was born into a poor family. At fourteen, he became seriously ill; when he recovered, he had lost his memory and became a beggar. Wandering around the marketplace, he would shout, "Peace will come to the nation." Whenever a new government official took office, Chou Tien would pay him a visit and say, "I bring news of good times."

At that time, the Mongols were the rulers of China. Afraid that their Han-Chinese subjects would rebel and overthrow them, the Mongols enforced martial law throughout the country. Possession of weapons became a major crime, and several families had to share one kitchen knife. Thus, when the people heard Chou Tien's ravings, they shook their heads and muttered, "This man is insane. How can he say that good times are coming when things are getting worse each day."

The Mongols' harsh rule began to stir up discontent. Eventually, rebellions broke out. One of the leaders of a peasant revolt was a man named Chu Yüan-chang. When Yüan-chang arrived in the town where Chou Tien was begging, Tien ran to meet him and shouted, "I bring news of good times." Yüan-chang was at first amused, but when Chou Tien continued to prophesy that peace and prosperity would come to the nation, he invited the mad beggar to accompany him on his military campaigns.

On the eve of a battle with a rival rebel leader named Chang Shih-ch'eng, Yüan-chang asked Chou Tien, "What are my chances of winning?"

Tien replied, "Your rival is not destined to become an emperor."

The next day, Yüan-chang went into battle with confidence and defeated Shih-ch'eng.

After Chu Yüan-chang became the new emperor of China, Chou Tien went to court to congratulate him. When Yüan-chang saw Tien, he said to himself, "If this man can help me win my throne, he can also help others take it from me. I must kill him before it's too late."

Chou Tien divined this and said, "Don't waste your time and effort trying to kill me. I cannot be harmed by fire, water, or weapons."

The emperor did not believe him. "Tie up the madman's hands and feet and throw him into the cauldron," Yüan-chang instructed his guards. "And make sure the fire underneath is hot."

After an hour or so, Chou Tien stood up inside the pot

and smiled; he was neither burned nor scalded. Yüan-chang then ordered his men to cover the cauldron with a heavy lid. "This will kill him for sure," said the emperor. "No one can survive being cooked for several hours."

The hours passed. There was no movement or noise inside the pot, so Chu Yüan-chang thought the diviner was finally dead. He opened the cauldron, looked inside, and saw Chou Tien sleeping like an infant. The emperor dropped the lid in shock. Chou Tien woke up, yawned, and said, "What was that noise that disturbed my sleep?"

After this incident, Chu Yüan-chang knew that he could not kill Tien. So he put him in a Buddhist monastery and told the monks to monitor the diviner's activities.

One day, the abbot of the monastery went to the emperor and exclaimed, "Chou Tien has been quarreling with the monks and has refused to eat for almost a month. He has also wreaked havoc throughout the monastery."

The emperor knew that Chou Tien was up to his old tricks. "I will see what I can do," he told the abbot.

When Chu Yüan-chang arrived at the monastery, Chou Tien greeted him at the gate and said, "The monks here are bored. I thought I'd liven them up with some entertainment."

Yüan-chang realized that it would be impossible to confine Tien or control his actions. So that evening, he invited his former adviser to a feast and said, "You have served me well. Name a gift and you shall have it."

Chou Tien replied seriously, "My lord emperor, I ask only that I may continue to enjoy myself in this world."

Chu Yüan-chang understood this request and formally released him from the monastery. "The man has no political ambitions," thought the emperor. "I don't think he'll be a threat to me after all." Chou Tien left the kingdom and disappeared into the forests of Mount Lu.

Toward the end of his reign, Chu Yüan-chang began to murder his former supporters, fearing they would overthrow him. Chou Tien was one of the few who escaped this purge.

CHOU TIEN helped Chu Yüan-chang end the Yüan dynasty (1271–1368 CE) of the Mongols and establish the Ming dynasty (1368–1644 CE).

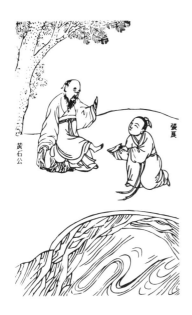

30
The Old Man and the Kingmaker
Huang-shih Kung and Chang Liang

The emperor of Ch'in united China, built the Great Wall, and crushed all possible opposition. His empire was expected to last ten thousand years.

In a small village far from the capital, a common citizen named Liu Pang was on his way to the herb shop to buy medicine for his mother. At the marketplace, Pang ran into

Huang-shih Kung (left) and Chang Liang.

an old man who looked at him and asked, "Why are you in a hurry? Your mother will not live to see nightfall."

Instead of being angry, Liu Pang asked respectfully, "Honored teacher, can you tell me about my future?"

The old man replied, "On the mountain south of the village there is a slab of stone pointing up to the sky. In front of it is a pool as clear as a mirror. When your mother dies, you should bury her between the stone and the water."

Liu Pang went home and stayed with his mother until she died that evening. As instructed by the old man, he took her coffin up the mountain, found the spot between the stone and the water, and buried her there.

In another village at sunrise, a young farmer was walking to his fields. As he approached the stone bridge at the edge of town, he heard someone call to him, "Young man, come here." The farmer looked in the direction of the voice and saw an old man sitting by the bridge.

"I've dropped my sandal down the riverbank," the old man said. "Can you pick it up for me?"

The farmer, whose name was Chang Liang, immediately went down the steep banks of the river and retrieved the shoe. He brought it to the old man who said, "Put it on for me. I can't bend down to tie the laces." Chang Liang fastened the sandal on the man's foot and was about to continue on his way when he heard the stranger say, "You are worthy of being taught. Come back tomorrow at sunrise."

Chang Liang arrived at the bridge the next morning at dawn. To his surprise, the old man was already sitting on the riverbank. As Liang approached him, the man got up and walked away. The next morning, Liang arrived at the bridge before sunrise but again the old man was already there, and again he turned and left when Liang tried to greet him.

That evening, Chang Liang said to himself, "I will go to the bridge and sit there throughout the night."

The next morning, when the old man saw Chang Liang waiting at the bridge, he said, "You are a worthy student. I will teach you everything you need to know to overthrow the cruel emperor."

The old man gave Chang Liang two books, one on military strategy and one on divination, saying, "Study them well. When you meet a man named Liu Pang, you should help him defeat the emperor of Ch'in. Liu Pang is destined to be the founder of the next dynasty. The place where his mother is buried is a 'kingmaker' site."

The old man continued, "There is one book that I won't give you yet. When you have finished your tasks, look for a yellow rock on Mount Ku. That is my home, for my name is Huang-shih Kung, the Old Man of the Yellow Rock."

Chang Liang spent several years studying the arts of military strategy and divination. He eventually met Liu Pang, became Pang's chief adviser, and helped him defeat the emperor of Ch'in.

After Liu Pang ascended the throne, he summoned Chang Liang and told him, "Without you, I could not have become the son of heaven."

The new emperor then graciously offered the diviner his choice of lands and titles, but Liang said, "My lord, I have no desire for either. However, I would be honored if you would give me the parcel of land where we first met. I would like to retire there with fond memories of our friendship."

The small town where Chiang Liang had met Liu Pang was located in one of the poorest regions of the empire.

The land was barren; the soil was stony; and the towns and villages were small and scattered.

Chang Liang knew that Liu Pang would eventually become jealous and suspicious of those who had helped him overthrow the Ch'in dynasty. If Liang had refused a reward, he would have offended his emperor. On the other hand, if he had requested rich lands near the capital, he would be singled out as a competitor to the throne. Therefore, wisely and tactfully, Chang Liang asked for a poor region far from the capital, citing reasons that flattered the emperor.

After receiving his gift, Liang retired from the government. He left the capital, journeyed to Mount Ku, and found the large yellow rock that Huang-shih Kung had described. Next to the rock was a book titled *The Arts of Longevity and Immortality,* and inside the book was a note that said, "This is the other book that I told you about. You are ready for it now."

Chang Liang took the book, went into the mountains, and was never seen again.

Toward the end of his life, Liu Pang did indeed come to fear that his ministers and military commanders would overthrow him and begin to murder his closest advisers. Of those who had helped the emperor gain the throne, only Chang Liang did not suffer a violent death.

HUANG-SHIH KUNG is a legendary figure from prehistoric China. He is the patron of diviners and feng-shui practitioners.

Chang Liang lived from the end of the Ch'in dynasty (221–207 BCE) to the early part of the Han dynasty (206 BCE–219 CE). He was chief adviser to Liu Pang and played a considerable role in ending the Ch'in dynasty and establishing that of the Han.

31
Master of
Ghost Valley

Kuei-ku Tzu

Kuei-ku Tzu's mother had always wanted a child, but her husband died before she could conceive. One night, she fell asleep by her husband's grave and dreamed that he came to lie with her. The next morning, she discovered she was pregnant. When the child was born, she named him Kuei-ku Tzu, which means "son of the Seed of a Ghost."

Kuei-ku Tzu was an extraordinary child. At sixteen, he had mastered the subjects of military strategy, divination, geography, and astronomy. He was also interested in the arts of longevity and immortality, and frequently went into the mountains to gather herbs and plants that he made into elixirs.

Kuei-ku Tzu was over a hundred years old when he set-tled in a place called Kuei-ku (Ghost Valley). It was to Ghost Valley that Sun Pin, the grandson of the great mili-tary strategist Sun Tzu, went to study strategy, tactics, and diplomacy. Soon, others also flocked to Ghost Valley to learn from this legendary teacher.

Kuei-ku Tzu was not only adept at statecraft and military strategy; he could also see into the hearts of his students and predict their future. To Sun Pin, he said, "You will meet with many hardships before you find peace and contentment."

Sun Pin became the military adviser of the lord of Ch'i until a jealous rival kidnapped and tortured him. Crippled and left to die in the wilderness, he finally realized that the political arena was fraught with dangers. Pin was lucky to be rescued by a woodcutter who nursed him back to health. After Sun Pin had regained his strength, he returned to Ghost Valley and lived out the rest of his days as a hermit. Of all the famous political and military advisers of the era, he was the only one who did not die a violent death.

To Pang Chüan, Kuei-ku Tzu said, "You have a ruthless nature. If you don't tame it, you will come to a violent end." Chüan was the jealous rival who tortured Sun Pin. Although he eventually became the top military adviser to the lord of Wei, he was killed on the battlefield.

Su Ch'in and Chang Yi were friends who journeyed to-gether to Ghost Valley to learn from Kuei-ku Tzu. To them, he said, "You are friends now, but will you forsake your friendship when you serve different lords?"

When Su Ch'in and Chang Yi completed their studies, Kuei-ku Tzu gave them this advice: "You will both become famous statesmen. However, even the most beautiful flowers of spring die in the autumn. Your desire for fame and prestige will be your downfall. If you don't retreat when your work is done, your lives will be brief, and you will never experience true happiness."

Su Ch'in became the chief adviser to the lord of Ch'i. His friend Chang Yi became adviser to the lord of Ch'in. In the war between the two states, the former friends became bitter enemies. When Ch'i was defeated by Ch'in, Su Ch'in was executed like the rest of the Ch'i ministers. The lord of Ch'in eventually crushed his rivals and united China. Chang Yi was deemed a dangerous competitor for the throne and was murdered soon after the lord of Ch'in became emperor of China.

KUEI-KU TZU lived during the latter part of the Chou dynasty (1122–221 BCE) in the era known as the Warring States (475–221 BCE). His teachings on statecraft, military science, and divination are collected in a book titled *Kuei-ku Tzu*.

32
Master of K'an-yu
Kuo P'u

Kuo P'u was born and raised in a town named East River. When he was nine years old, he met a diviner named Kuo Kung. Seeing that the boy was destined to become a master of the arcane arts, the old man taught Kuo P'u the *I-ching*, the theories of yin and yang, the five elements, and the art of k'an-yu (feng-shui). *K'an* means "high places," or "mountains," and *yu* means "low places," or "valleys." Thus, k'an-yu is the art and science of reading the patterns of energy in the mountains and valleys.

While most young men of his age aspired to government posts, Kuo P'u was uninterested in a career in the civil service. He was unkempt and undisciplined, and spent most of his time drinking and writing poetry. Often, he would leave his home for weeks or even months to walk in the mountains or float down the rivers.

To most people, Kuo P'u was an eccentric who had no patience for social conventions. Only P'u's closest friends knew that he was a master diviner who could read omens in the sky, sea, and land. Thus, when he predicted that the town of East River would be sacked by bandits, his friends heeded his words: they sold their properties, packed up their goods, and left. A month later, the river overflowed its banks and flooded the city. While the soldiers from the garrison were off repairing the dams, robbers looted the town.

When Kuo P'u's mother died, he buried her in a sandy beach a hundred paces from the river's edge. The feng-shui masters laughed at him and said, "The site will be flooded and all the fortunes of her descendants will be washed away."

P'u countered, "This land will become grassland within our children's lifetime, and when the soil and natural vegetation change, the Kuo family fortunes will change for the better."

Kuo P'u did not live to see the changes, but a generation later, the river had deposited enough silt for grass to grow near the grave. Although P'u had been poor all his life, the family fortunes took a dramatic turn during his son's generation. His sons and nephews became wealthy merchants, and Kuo P'u's works on feng-shui were acknowledged as authoritative treatises on selecting burial sites.

Once, when he was helping a friend select a site for a new house, P'u examined several plots and finally found one to his liking. He turned to his friend and said, "This piece of land will soon be blessed by the energy of the dragon. Within ten days, your fortunes will change for the better."

The emperor happened to be visiting the region disguised as a common citizen. Hearing Kuo P'u's evaluation of the land, he was unhappy. Common citizens were not allowed to own land with dragon energy; only the emperor and his closest relatives could build homes on such plots. The emperor immediately went to Kuo P'u's friend and said, "Do you know that it is a capital crime to build a home on land with dragon energy?"

"Yes, I do," replied the man. "But Master Kuo did not say that this land had dragon energy. Rather, he said that this land will be blessed by the energy of the dragon. And by that he meant that I will be blessed by the emperor when he visits my home." Just then, a messenger arrived from the capital. He prostrated himself before the emperor and announced, "Your majesty, there are matters at the palace that require your immediate attention."

When the neighbors heard that Kuo P'u's friend had been visited by the emperor, word began to spread. Soon gifts from the mayor and the town elders arrived to honor the "friend" of the emperor.

When Kuo P'u was about forty years old, he divined that he would soon die violently. From that day on, he locked himself in his study and wrote down his lifetime's research on divination, feng-shui, and the *I-ching*. Not long after P'u had completed his books, he offended the warlord Wang Tun and was executed.

Three days after the execution, Kuo P'u was seen eating and drinking at his favorite restaurant. When this was reported to Wang Tun, the warlord ordered that P'u's grave be opened and examined. In front of a large crowd of witnesses and curious onlookers, the examiners dug up the coffin and removed the lid. To the astonishment of everyone, the coffin was empty. It was only then that the people realized that Kuo P'u was a master of the arcane arts who was not only able to release his spirit just before death, but could "borrow" his body back now and then to walk in the earthly realm.

KUO P'U lived during the Chin dynasty (265–420 CE). He was a diviner, geographer, astronomer, mythologist, and poet. His book on the selection of burial sites, titled *Chuang-shu (The Burial Classic)*, is still widely studied by modern feng-shui practitioners.

33

The Reader of Dynastic Destiny

Lin Ling-su

The legends say that on the night Lin Ling-su was conceived, his mother dreamed that she saw an immortal who
said, "I would like to live here for a while." When Ling-su
was born, a golden light hovered over the chamber and the
scent of blossoms filled the air. His mother knew that her
son was no ordinary child, but when he still didn't speak at
the age of five, she was worried. She consulted all the doc-
tors in town but none could help her.

One day, a Taoist arrived at her home and asked to see

her son. When Ling-su saw the Taoist, he shouted excitedly, "It's been a long time since we last saw each other!"

From that time on, Ling-su began to speak. A year later, he began to write poetry. By age eight, he had become an expert in the Taoist and Confucian classics.

The great poet Su Tung-po heard about Ling-su's talent and paid him a visit.

"I have a gift for you," said the poet, as he handed the child a book on divination. Ling-su flipped through the pages, closed the book, and recited the contents from memory.

Su Tung-po was shocked. He sighed and said, "Your intelligence far surpasses mine. Fame and fortune await you on the horizon."

Surprisingly, Ling-su said, "Whether you are a noble or a commoner, rich or poor, famous or unknown—at best you'll end up as a ghost. My destiny lies beyond this."

When Lin Ling-su was twelve, he met an immortal who taught him the arts of magic and divination. Within two years Ling-su had learned everything the Taoist could teach him. On parting, Ling-su's teacher told him, "You now have the power to command the elements, drive out evil spirits, and see into the future. Use your abilities to benefit others and do not abuse your power. You will soon meet the emperor at the gates of the Celestial Palace. See that you advise him well."

The Sung emperor was a devout Taoist. One night, he traveled in spirit to the celestial realm to ask for an audience with the lords of heaven. At the gates of the Celestial Palace, he was met by an immortal who told him, "I have been sent by the lords of heaven to give you this message: listen to the advice of honest and virtuous ministers. Stay away from those who speak falsely. Only in this way can your kingdom be saved."

On the way back to his palace, the emperor met the same immortal, this time riding on a blue ox. The immortal dismounted, bowed before the emperor, and simply said, "Your majesty!"

When the emperor woke up the next morning, he summoned the court priest and said, "Introduce me to the most virtuous Taoist in my kingdom."

The priest responded, "You should meet Lin Ling-su."

When Ling-su arrived at the palace, the emperor looked at him and inquired, "What are your abilities?"

Lin Ling-su replied, "I can travel to the celestial realm; I can predict the future of humanity; and I can intercede on behalf of the dead. Not long ago, we met in the celestial realm."

The emperor was delighted, but he wanted to test Ling-su some more. So he said, "Now I remember the incident. Where's your blue ox?"

"It's grazing in the green meadows of a foreign country," Ling-su answered. "If it pleases your majesty, I can send word to have it brought here." The next spring, a delegation from Korea arrived at the Sung court and presented a gift—the blue ox—to the Chinese emperor.

The emperor was so impressed with Lin Ling-su that he invited the Taoist to be his spiritual adviser and gave him a large stipend of gold and cloth.

Ling-su's friendship with the emperor soon aroused jealousy among the ministers. One of them, T'sai Ching, decided to slander his rival. "Ling-su secretly wants to sit on the throne," T'sai Ching told the emperor. "He sleeps in a golden bed decorated with dragons and wears the nine-dragons robe. He won't allow people to visit him because he doesn't want his ambitions to be known."

The emperor said, "Then we should go and see if this is true."

The two men went to Ling-su's retreat and looked through a window. All they saw was a wooden bed, a table, and several benches. T'sai Ching knew that he was in trouble. Quickly, he fell at the emperor's feet and asked for forgiveness. "I only reported what others told me," he said.

When Lin Ling-su heard the commotion outside, he opened the door and said, "It is an honor to have your majesty visit my humble dwelling. Please come in."

The emperor asked Ling-su for forgiveness, saying, "I was told that you had adorned your retreat as if you were an emperor. Please forgive me." He then looked at T'sai Ching and said, "I should not have believed your lies."

The years passed, and the Sung emperor began to forget Ling-su's advice. He neglected his duties as the protector of his people and began to rely on his ministers to rule the country.

One night, Lin Ling-su looked up at the sky and saw the emperor's guardian star weakening while another star rose in the north. He sighed and said to himself, "It is written in the heavens. The emperor has lost his mandate to rule. A new ruler is rising to power in the north. There's nothing left for me to do."

The next morning, Lin Ling-su asked for permission to leave. Unable to retain him, the emperor thanked the Taoist for his service and gave him three hundred pounds of gold. When T'sai Ching, who had by then become the chief minister, discovered that Ling-su had received this great gift from the emperor, he told his personal guard, "Kill Ling-su and take his gold."

Ling-su divined T'sai Ching's evil intentions. He returned the three hundred pounds of gold to the emperor. The next day, when the assassins arrived at his retreat, the Taoist was nowhere to be found.

After leaving the capital, Lin Ling-su retreated into the mountains. There he gathered a group of students and taught them the arts of longevity. One day, he called his students together and said, "The country is about to be plunged into war. You should hide in the mountains and wait for the storm to pass. As for me, my time in the mortal realm is over, and I must return to where I originally came from."

Ling-su then sat in a meditation posture, closed his eyes, and sent his spirit to the celestial realm. Not long afterward, the Chin tribe invaded the Sung empire from the north and captured the emperor. Eventually, this tribe was conquered by the Mongols, who swept south and brought an end to the Sung dynasty.

LIN LING-SU lived during the latter part of the Sung dynasty (960–1279 CE). It is said that he predicted the kidnapping of the Sung emperor and the fall of the dynasty.

PART FIVE

Alchemists

34

The Master of
Spirit Travel

Chang Po-tuan

Chang Po-tuan was interested in Buddhism and Taoism even when he was child. He read any book he could get ahold of, but his favorite texts were those on meditation and the arts of longevity.

Not attracted to a career in the civil service, Po-tuan went to the T'ien-tai Mountains to study meditation with a Buddhist monk.

When he was almost sixty years old, Chang Po-tuan met a Taoist from Szechwan by the name of Liu Hai-ch'an and began to practice the Taoist techniques of cultivating body and mind.

Po-tuan had a friend who was a Zen Buddhist. The two men often met to meditate together and discuss Buddhist and Taoist philosophy. One day, the friend, whose Buddhist name was Hui-ting, went to Po-tuan's retreat and said, "I have mastered the technique of spirit travel. When I enter meditative stillness, I can send my spirit anywhere I want."

Po-tuan proposed, "Shall we travel somewhere together today?"

"My pleasure!" replied Hui-ting.

"Where shall we go?" asked Po-tuan.

"How about the gardens in Yang county?" suggested his friend. "I've heard that the flowers there are beautiful at this time of year."

The two men sat on their meditation cushions, closed their eyes, and sent their spirits to the flower gardens of Yang county. When Po-tuan arrived, he found his friend already sitting on a bench. Hui-ting remarked, "I've already walked around the garden three times."

Po-tuan only said, "Why don't we each take a flower back as a souvenir?"

Hui-ting nodded. The friends walked through the garden and each plucked a flower.

Back in Po-tuan's retreat, the two men opened their eyes and stretched their legs.

"Where's your flower?" Po-tuan asked his friend. Hui-ting could not find his. Po-tuan then reached into his sleeve and brought out a beautiful chrysanthemum.

At first, Hui-ting was disappointed, but then he laughed and said, "I'm glad one of us was able to bring back a flower." Po-tuan gave the flower to his friend and said, "I know you appreciate flowers. Take this one home in memory of the good time we had today."

Later, when Hui-ting had left, Po-tuan's students asked, "Why couldn't Hui-ting bring back a flower?"

Their teacher replied, "Hui-ting cultivated his mind alone. Therefore, when he entered stillness, he could liberate only his spirit. As a result, the entire journey was in his mind. On the other hand, I cultivate both mind and body. When my spirit travels, it can take on corporeal form and influence reality. That's why I could bring back a flower and he couldn't."

When Chang Po-tuan was about to shed his body and enter the immortal realm, he called his students together and said, "After I have gone, you should cremate my body." At ninety-nine years of age, he sent his spirit into the immortal realm. After the students cremated his body, they found among the ashes thousands of tiny fragments of bones that glowed with a golden hue.

CHANG PO-TUAN lived during the early part of the Sung dynasty (960–1279 CE). He is one of the greatest exponents of the Southern Complete Reality School and is the author of the famous internal-alchemical classic *Wu-chen p'ien (Understanding Reality)*.

35
The Father of
T'ai-Chi Ch'uan
Chang San-feng

Chang San-feng's original name was Chang Chun-pao. His parents were poor, so they sent him to the Shaolin Buddhist monastery to become a monk.

Chun-pao was a talented apprentice: by fourteen, he had mastered the Shaolin martial arts, as well as Zen meditation. However, despite these accomplishments, he felt that there was something missing in his training. Thus, at the age of fifteen, he decided to leave Shaolin to look for other teachers.

During his travels, Chun-pao met an immortal named

Huo-lung (Fire Dragon) who taught him the arts of gathering, cultivating, and circulating internal energy.

As Chun-pao's cultivation progressed, his appearance changed. His head began to resemble that of a tortoise and his bones became as light as a crane's. His ears grew and his eyes shone with an inner glow. Summer and winter, he wore a hemp robe and straw sandals.

Chang Chun-pao visited many famous mountains where Taoist hermits had settled, but did not find a place to his liking. Once, when he was a guest at the Golden Altar Monastery, he fell asleep and did not wake up for a month. Thinking that he had passed away, his friends bought a casket and performed the funeral rites. Suddenly, Chun-pao sat up and demanded, "Why have you put me in a coffin?"

After this incident, he went to Szechwan and settled on Mount T'ai-ho. He built a hut in the shelter of an ancient grove and spent much of his time in meditation. By then, he was immune to hunger and thirst.

One day, Chang Chun-pao heard a commotion outside his retreat. He looked out of the window and saw a monkey and a snake fighting in front of his hut. As he watched the movements of the combatants, he saw that while the snake had the advantage of speed and flexibility, the monkey had the advantage of agility. "Each animal has its natural ability to defend itself," he observed. "If humans could learn the best of each animal's style of fighting and combine them into one form, what a powerful form of martial art that would be!"

For several years, Chun-pao worked hard to develop a martial art that combined the fighting abilities of various animals. However, after he had created a seemingly invincible fighting style, he still felt it was incomplete.

One day, while walking in the Wu-tang Mountains,

Chang Chun-pao looked into a valley and saw leaves whipped into a spiral by the wind. He then looked at the sky and saw clouds swirling around the jagged peaks. Finally, he realized that the forces of the Tao far outweigh the abilities of animals and humans and said to himself, "The aim of the martial arts is not to subdue and conquer opposing forces but to dissolve, deflect, and absorb them."

Chang Chun-pao built a hermitage in the Wu-tang Mountains and began to develop another form of martial art, one based on neutralizing and transforming opposing forces. Using the principles of the Tao as manifested in nature, he called the method T'ai-Ch'i Ch'uan.

One day, while wandering around the mountains of Wu-tang, Chang Chun-pao saw a rock formation that resembled three peaks pointing up to the sky. Taken by the view, he said, "From now on, my name will be Chang San-feng (Three Peaks)."

Chang San-feng lived in the mountains for twenty-three years. One day, when he was about a hundred years old, he suddenly left his hermitage and was never seen again.

CHANG SAN-FENG lived from the end of the Yüan dynasty (1271–1368 CE) into the Ming dynasty (1368–1644 CE). He founded the Wu-tang sect, wrote numerous treatises on internal alchemy, and is considered by many to be the originator of T'ai-Chi Ch'uan.

36
The Woman Who Could Turn Minerals into Gold
Cheng Wei's Wife

Cheng Wei loved the Taoist alchemical arts and married a woman with similar interests. The couple built two laboratories in a quiet corner of their estate where, in their spare time, they would experiment with making the pill of immortality and turning mercury into gold.

One day, Cheng Wei hurried home and said to his wife, "The emperor has invited all the officials of this district to a banquet, and I don't have a proper robe for the occasion.

Even if we bought the materials immediately, I don't think we could get someone to finish it in time. What should I do? My whole career in the government depends on this audience with the emperor."

His wife answered, "Don't worry. The robe will be ready for you immediately." She waved her arm and two bolts of satin materialized on the table. When she pointed at the cloth, the material was transformed into an elegant robe.

Cheng Wei was very happy, but secretly he was jealous of his wife's magical abilities.

Another time, Cheng Wei had worked all night in his laboratory trying to transform mercury into gold and had gotten no results. Returning to his room tired and disappointed, he happened to walk past his wife's laboratory. As he looked through the window, he saw something gleaming in her hands. Bursting into his wife's laboratory, Cheng Wei cried, "You have had the secrets of making gold all this time and didn't tell me!"

His wife replied, "To succeed in the arts of alchemy, it must be in your destiny." She turned and walked away, leaving him angry and frustrated.

Cheng Wei tried to entice his wife with money and jewels, hoping that she would give him the formula. When she refused, he went to a friend and said, "My wife knows the formula for transforming mercury into gold and will not tell me. If you can figure out how to get the formula from her, I'll make sure you're rich for the rest of your life."

The friend came up with a plan: they would poison the woman and then threaten to withhold the antidote if she did not reveal the formula. However, Cheng Wei's wife discovered the plot. She confronted her husband and said to him, "The secrets of the Tao are transmitted only to the right person, even if you only meet him casually on the street. If the person is unsuitable, the Tao is not transmitted, even if refusal means death."

That evening, Cheng Wei's wife smeared mud over her face, feigned madness, and ran away from home naked. Her husband chased her to the edge of town, but she vanished into the night.

Later, the townspeople reported seeing a madwoman in shabby clothes flying up to the sky. Cheng Wei spent the rest of his life experimenting with making a pill of immortality and turning mercury into gold. He succeeded in neither.

CHENG WEI'S wife lived during the latter part of the Han dynasty (206 BCE–219 CE). Not much is known about her except that her maiden name was Fang and she was an adept alchemist.

葛洪

37
The Sage Who Embraced Simplicity
Ko Hung

Ko Hung was attracted to the arts of immortality even when he was a child. His family was poor, so he had to collect branches and sell them as firewood in order to buy books and paper. Every evening, after his family had retired to bed, Ko Hung would stay up long into the night studying the classics of medicine, divination, and immortality.

At eighteen, Ko Hung had earned himself the reputation of the most learned scholar in his town. When his family and friends tried to persuade him to enter the civil service, he replied that he was not interested. Hung moved out of his village, built a hut in the mountains, and lived the life of a hermit.

He rarely spoke, did not receive guests, and was not interested in the bustle and excitement of town life. Daily, he studied the Taoist classics and the arts of longevity and immortality. When he had problems understanding a text, Hung would travel hundreds of miles to find a teacher to explain the teachings to him.

On one of his journeys, Ko Hung heard about an alchemist named Cheng Yin and traveled a thousand miles to Yin's retreat to ask for instruction.

"I do not accept students," said Cheng Yin. "However, because you are sincere and willing to learn, I'll make an exception this time."

At the end of Hung's apprenticeship, Yin said to his student, "I have taught you everything I know. If you want to continue your studies, you should find a man named Pao Hsüan. He is the magistrate of the county of Nan Hai."

Ko Hung set out for Nan Hai, found Pao Hsüan, and asked to be accepted as a student. Although Hsüan was a government official, he had a deep interest in medicine, alchemy, divination, astronomy, geography, and magic, and was an expert in all these areas of learning.

On their first meeting, Pao Hsüan was so impressed with Ko Hung that he not only accepted Hung as his student, but decided to make him his son-on-law.

When Ko Hung heard that Mount Lao Fao was rich in cinnabar and other alchemical ingredients, he went to the magistrate of that area and said, "I would be grateful if you could give me a minor post in a village near Mount Lao Fao."

The magistrate could not understand why the young man would want an assignment in a remote and mountainous area. "People with your abilities and background should apply for a post in a large city. No one will notice you in a small village," he protested.

Ko Hung replied, "I'm not interested in a career in the civil service. All I want is to live in an area where I can gather herbs and minerals to make the pill of immortality."

The magistrate now understood Hung's wishes. He appointed him supervisor of public works in a village at the foot of Mount Lao Fao and gave him a stipend of grain and cloth. Ko Hung lived there for seven years. He built a laboratory, set up a furnace and a cauldron, and went into the mountains daily to collect the ingredients needed for making the pill of immortality.

When Ko Hung was eighty-one years old, he wrote a letter to his friend Teng Yüeh saying, "I will be leaving soon to find teachers who can show me the path to immortality." Realizing that Hung was alluding to his departure from the mortal realm, Yüeh set out immediately for Mount Lao Fao, hoping to see his friend one more time.

Yüeh arrived at Ko Hung's retreat and found him sitting on the bed. Hung's eyes were closed, a golden glow radiated from his body, and a sweet fragrance filled the room. When Teng Yüeh saw green and red vapors floating around the cauldron, he realized that Hung had succeeded in making the Dragon-Tiger Elixir.

Teng Yüeh kept a vigil at his friend's home for three days. When the light and the fragrance had disappeared, he went to make arrangements to have Ko Hung buried. However, when Yüeh returned with the undertaker and a coffin, Hung's body was nowhere to be found.

Ko Hung lived during the latter part of the Chin dynasty (265–420 CE) and is regarded as one of the greatest alchemists of his time. His book, the *Pao-p'u Tzu (The Sage Who Embraces Simplicity),* is still considered an authoritative text on the arts of longevity and immortality.

38
The Poet Immortal
Pai Yü-ch'an

Pai Yü-ch'an's original name was Ko Chang-keng. His father died when he was young, and after his mother remarried, Chang-keng changed his name to Pai Yü-ch'an.

Yü-ch'an not only was adept at art, calligraphy, and poetry, but was also a scholar. By seven, he had memorized the major Confucian and Taoist classics, and he was proclaimed a child prodigy by the local examiners at twelve. However, despite his talent, Yü-ch'an was not interested in pursuing a career in the government. At sixteen, he left home and wandered around southern China, looking for teachers to instruct him in the arts of longevity and immortality.

After several years of traveling, Pai Yü-ch'an decided to settle on Mount Lao Fao. There, he met a Taoist named Chen Ni-wan who accepted him as a student. Yü-ch'an studied with Ni-wan for nine years. At the end of his apprenticeship, Ni-wan told him, "You are learning so fast that I thought something was unusual. Last night, I went to the celestial realm and discovered that you were once an immortal. Because you offended the lords of heaven with your drunken behavior, you were condemned to spend time in the mortal realm, where you are to redeem yourself by leading people to the Tao. I was sent to help you to return to the celestial realm. Now my work is done. Make good use of your time in the mortal lands."

Ni-wan gave Pai Yü-ch'an a seal with the power to command thunder and lightning and then taught him how to return to the immortal realm. Yü-ch'an thanked his teacher, and the two men bowed to each other in farewell. Suddenly, Ni-wan turned around, walked to the edge of the cliff, and jumped into the river.

After leaving Mount Lao Fao, Pai Yü-ch'an traveled throughout the country, teaching the arts of immortality to anyone who was willing to learn.

One day, Yü-ch'an and three students were crossing a lake in a small boat when a fog rolled in. The boatman appealed to Pai Yü-ch'an, "Taoist teacher, can you help me find the pier? If we don't dock soon, the passengers will panic and the boat will capsize."

Calmly, Pai Yü-ch'an took a writing brush out of his sleeve, drew a picture of a moon on a piece of paper, and tossed it up to the sky. Immediately, the fog dispersed and a bright moon appeared. Guided by the moonlight, the boatman found the pier and steered the boat safely to shore.

When news of Pai Yü-ch'an's abilities reached the capital, the Sung emperor invited the Taoist to his court.

"Stay in my palace and be my adviser," said the emperor. Yü-ch'an was not interested in being a "court Taoist," so he said, "My home is among the cranes and the white clouds."

One year, Pai Yü-ch'an decided to celebrate the Autumn Moon Festival by the river with his friends. The group was laughing, drinking, and making poetry when suddenly Pai Yü-ch'an stood up and jumped into the water. Just as his friends were about to dive in to save him, Yü-ch'an's head surfaced. He looked at his friends, shook his head, indicating that they were not to rescue him, and then disappeared into the depths of the river. Pai Yü-ch'an, like his teacher Chen Ni-wan, had chosen to shed his shell in the water when he sent his spirit to the immortal realm.

PAI YÜ-CH'AN lived during the latter part of the Sung dynasty (960–1279 CE). He is the fifth patriarch of the Southern Complete Reality School. His writings on the arts of longevity and immortality are collected in the *Pai Yü-ch'an ch'üan-chi* (*The Collected Works of Pai Yü-ch'an*).

39
Lady of the Great Yin
T'ai-yin Nü

T'ai-yin Nü loved the Taoist arts of immortality from the time she was a child. When she could not find someone to instruct her, she said to herself, "I'll study by myself. If it is in my destiny, then someday I'll find a teacher."

The years passed, and T'ai-yin Nü still had not found a teacher. "I'll set up a wine shop in the marketplace," she thought. "Maybe I'll meet a teacher there."

Several more years went by. Nü waited patiently. She built a retreat at the edge of town and spent her spare time meditating and experimenting with elixirs of immortality.

One morning, a man came to her shop to buy a flask of wine. Noticing that the woman who served him was well mannered and intelligent, he said, "You walk the path of the white tiger and snake; I walk the path of the green dragon and black tortoise. In this world, who can understand this?"

When T'ai-yin Nü heard this, she was delighted. She asked the man, "What is the numeric of the element earth?"

He replied, "I don't know the numeric of the element earth, but south is three, north is five, east is nine, west is seven, and the center is one."

"You are a man of honor and virtue," exclaimed Nü. "I asked you about one thing and you gave me answers for five. Please come to my hermitage for a meal and tell me more about the Tao."

T'ai-yin Nü closed her shop and boarded up the windows; she knew that she would never return to the marketplace.

That evening during dinner, her guest said to her, "My name is T'ai-yang Tzu and I am a subordinate of the celestial lords. I have drunk the water of the sacred light; I have ascended to the North Star; and my body has the five treasures. In acknowledging me as a virtuous man, you have become a part of my family."

T'ai-yang Tzu stayed at T'ai-yin Nü's retreat for several days and taught her the arts of immortality. Before he left, he told her, "Continue to practice your meditation. Fly to the stars to receive instructions from the celestial lords. They will let you know when the elixir is ready."

One day, T'ai-yin Nü saw a purple vapor rising from the cauldron. Intuitively she knew the elixir was ready. She poured it into a cup, drank it, and floated up to the sky. At that time, she was almost two hundred years old, but her appearance resembled that of a young woman.

T'AI-YIN NÜ probably lived during the T'ang dynasty (618–906 CE). Not much else is known about her.

40
Father of
Immortal Alchemy
Wei Po-yang

Wei Po-yang was a native of southeast China. Even as a child, he was attracted to the alchemical arts of immortality. At the age of eighteen, he went into the mountains, built a laboratory, and experimented with making the pill of immortality.

Po-yang had three students. Two were intelligent and devious; the third was dim-witted but sincere. The master knew that his intelligent students were suspicious and

Wei Po-yang (left), the trusting student, and the dog.

greedy: they only wanted to attain immortality and did not care how they did it. So, when he succeeded in making the pill of immortality, he decided to test his three apprentices.

Wei Po-yang called his students together and said, "I think I have succeeded in making the pill of immortality, but before we take it, we should test it on the dog."

Po-yang opened the lid of the cauldron, took out one of the pills, and gave it to the dog. Minutes later, the dog fell over and stopped breathing. Wei Po-yang sighed and said, "It is the will of heaven."

The two intelligent students looked at each other, then at their teacher, and said, "It looks like we've failed again." Wei Po-yang replied, "The pill may have a different effect on humans. We won't know its true effect until one of us takes it."

When none of the students volunteered, Wei Po-yang said, "I will give it a try." After swallowing the pill, he too fell down and stopped breathing.

The two intelligent students said to each other, "Our teacher has died from this pill. It would be stupid for us to take it and die as well. After all, our goal is to attain immortality. If we can't become immortal, then we should go home." They went into the laboratory, gathered their belongings, and made their way down the mountain.

The dim-witted student stood and looked at the cauldron for a long time. Then he said to himself, "My teacher has always been a cautious man. He wouldn't take a pill that would kill him." Slowly, he reached into the cauldron, picked up a pill, and swallowed it. Then he sat on a rock and waited. Suddenly, Wei Po-yang stood up, laughed, and patted the student on his back. Moments later, the dog also stood up and ran to his master.

Wei Po-yang soon began to feel weightless. When he

took a step, he found himself floating up to the sky. Flying up close behind him were his student and the dog. The three were spotted by the apprentices who had decided to leave their teacher. The two students hurried back to the laboratory, but when they got there, the fire in the furnace was out and there was nothing left in the cauldron.

WEI PO-YANG lived during the latter part of the Han dynasty (206 BCE–219 CE). He is regarded as the father of the alchemical arts of immortality and is the author of the first Taoist alchemical text, *Tsan-tung-chi (Triplex Unity)*.